SADDAM

And ME

Dr Mosa Abu-Rgheff

Table of Contents

Chapter 1

To most people, Iraq is a dry, arid country, unable to support vegetation of any kind. I, however, know otherwise. My first memories arise from when my family and I lived in the Dujaila region, where the River Tigris breathes life into the country, producing rich, fertile land that's perfect for agriculture and orchards, which is the setting for many of my earliest memories.

I wasn't born in Dujaila. No, my parents moved there in 1950, from a city called Al-Hay, which is situated on the banks of the Al-Gharaf river. Al-Hay is about 40 km from Al-Kut, the main city in the region and is not far south of Baghdad. Al-Hay agricultural land produced the finest quality wheat, corn; sesame and sunflower which are all grown there.

I should say a few words about Dujaila and why my parents decided to move there from Al-Hay. Back in the 1930s, the Tigris' water level used to fluctuate depending on the time of year. As the local population is mostly farmers, they needed a constant flow all year round to keep things running smoothly. So the government's answer was to build a barrage on the river Tigris on the banks of Kut city. This was the purpose of the Dujalia project. Work started in 1934 and steady progress was made until 1939, when the war held things up for six years.

There were around 100 settler families initially. They were each given a plot of land to farm, 62 acres in total, which was divided up into 50 acres for food production and the rest for a family house, animal shelters and orchards. There were no buses or supermarkets in those days. Everyone lived off the land and if the crops failed, they starved, it's as simple as that.

So this is what attracted my parents to the area. I was four years old at the time, but I can still remember the sweet smell of fruit and the gushing noise produced by the river in the background. It became the backdrop to what would become the best years of my life. I come from what people in the West would deem to be a huge family. There were ten of us in total, 4 girls and 6 boys. I was the sixth of my siblings to be born.

Shortly after we moved, I started school. The local primary school was 2 km away, but, from a young age, I considered it to be a worthwhile trek. Not that it was a trek, not really.

Every day we got up early to the sound of birds singing outside and voices in the neighbouring fields. The rippling Tigris was ever-present in the background, but sometimes it was louder than others, depending on the time of year and the weather.

So, after a good breakfast, cooked using food that we had grown ourselves, we set off, full of enthusiasm for the coming day. I'll never forget those first few years of my schooling life.

At first, I looked over my shoulder occasionally, to see if my mother was still stood at the door, waiting for us to disappear from view. We noticed neighbours in the adjacent fields, some of whom waved and shouted good morning across the fields of golden crops. Sometimes we stopped to say hello to the cattle, who usually approached us more out of curiosity than any sense of recognition, we always used to feel.

Eventually, I'd turn round and see that my mother had gone inside, at which point I felt sad and liberated at the same time. That's when the chatter started up and my brother and I would find ourselves deep in conversation. It was during those walks to school that I really got to know my siblings, who were all older than me to begin with and, rather than feeling like the baby of the family, I felt like I could hold my own and be taken seriously, regardless of the topic of conversation.

We sometimes quarrelled, as all siblings do, but by the time the school building came into view, it was forgotten.

Each of us liked school, but on the way home, things felt just a bit more relaxed. We shared a few jokes and started talking about what our parents might have in store for us. In summer, the orchards were in bloom and I often paused, tempted to take a plump grape for myself. My brother would see me looking and shake his head, because we knew that as tempting as it was to help ourselves, people relied on the orchards to generate income for the winter, when living off the land wasn't so easy.

But it's summertime that provides my most vivid memories, with the sun beating down, burning our faces and making us perspire. Butterflies fluttered in the breeze and the fields around us were full of insects making all kinds of strange noises.

It was during one of these walks home that my older brother first brought up the subject of science, I forget the details, right now, but from then on, it was all I wanted to talk about.

There was only one school in the village, so all the neighbours' children went home the same way. Occasionally they'd join us, and we'd walk together. I enjoyed this, because it was a chance to get to know new people and hear alternative viewpoints on things that mattered to us. But on the other hand, there was no longer any sense of intimacy between my brothers and I, meaning it wasn't possible to talk about scientific issues or what our parents had been up to.

Then in 1954, when I was eight years old, my brother Hussein arrived on the scene. It's funny, because I knew right away that we were going to be good friends. I could just tell from the way he grinned when our eyes locked, and that lit up a fire in me that would grow stronger as we got older.

Eight years is a big difference between siblings, and it meant that by the time he was making the 2 km journey to school each day, I'd moved on to secondary school, which was in the nearby city.

It was often dark when I got back an hour or so later than my younger siblings. That didn't stop me from strengthening my bond with Hussein though. After we'd eaten, I used to sit with him for a couple of hours, helping him with his studies and chatting about whatever topic came to mind. In summer we'd go outside and listen to the sounds of the fields until the red sun began to near the horizon and the fading light made it impossible for us to carry on.

As the only school in the locality was the primary school I'd attended, I had to travel further afield to secondary school, to the nearest town, where I studied mainly science subjects.

These were happy days and, as I sat looking out at the fields with Hussein, I'd secretly wish they could last forever. Then, slowly but surely, things began to change. First of all, our plentiful bounty of delicious, nutritious food began to decrease. Whereas at one time, our plates had been overflowing, my siblings and I were being served up less and less.

There was something different about our parents too. My dad looked constantly worried and they started to have arguments for the first time ever. Then when my eldest brother sat

7

down and communicated to me his theory about why there was less food, we knew our time in Dujalia was drawing to an end.

It came as no surprise then, when in 1961, my dad announced we were moving to Baghdad, adding that, because the food produced by the land had been in decline, they had no choice in the matter.

As reluctant as I was to move, I understood that it was a case of needs must. It took a while to settle in, but once I had started at the Central Baghdad School, everything began to feel routine. My brothers found jobs in no time and my own studies went from strength to strength. A year later, my grades were so good that I was offered a government scholarship to study engineering. As excited as this made me, it paled in comparison to how I felt when I learnt they were going to fund a further year's study, and I'd be living in the UK.

I enjoyed my time studying engineering, and, in hindsight, it flew by far too quickly. I did my very best and achieved everything that was expected of me, but all I really wanted to do was climb aboard the plane to Heathrow.

The minute I got off the plane, I folded my arms and rubbed opposite shoulders to try and conceal the fact that I was shivering. I'd only just arrived and the last thing I wanted was to offend anyone for suggesting the climate was on the cold side.

However, secretly, I was just too cold to go anywhere, so I found a hotel in London and stayed there for a couple of days while I found some warm clothes for a price that I could afford.

The cities back home were busy, and I thought I'd never go anywhere as hectic as Baghdad, but I was wrong. In London, there are people everywhere and you have to fight your way through crowds to get to whatever it is you want to buy. As I was still a country boy at heart, this was something that took some getting used to.

Just two days following my arrival, I got the underground to Paddington. From there I caught a train to Swindon, where my sixth form college was located.

Dr Mosa Abu Rgheff

As I was queuing up to register for my A
levels, reading the multitude of forms that I'd
been asked to complete, I observed the excited,
chattering English people of around my age and
wondered how I was going to fit in. Things are
undoubtedly very different in England and part of
me worried that I'd soon be exposed, but I took
comfort in the knowledge that I was at the very
least going to hold my own when it came to
academic work.

I mostly enjoyed my time at Swindon, in fact,
I would go so far as to say that the signing up
process was the worst part of it. A year into my
studies, I started considering what I was going to
do next and decided upon a degree in Electrical
and Electronic Engineering at the University of
Leeds. They had strict entry requirements, but
when they informed me of the grades I needed, I
never once doubted myself. As it happened, I
attained the required number of UCAS points and
then some.

Chapter 2

I remember how everyone was in such high spirits on the day our results came out. Now, I'm not a party guy, never have been, but it's safe to say that I let my hair down a bit, a bit more than usual, that night.

I wasn't the only one amongst my circle of friends to attain the required grades. In fact, almost all of us did.

We decided to go out for a meal a couple of nights later, not just to celebrate but also to mark the end of an era. As I was preparing to leave the house, the thought struck me for the first time that I probably wasn't going to be seeing many of them again. We'd been through a lot together over the previous couple of years, and the sudden onset of sobriety felt a bit like a coming of age moment. I sat on my bed for a few moments, contemplating. I asked myself if there was a lesson to be learnt that was actually the real takeaway from studying away from home.

I slept soundly that night. When I woke up, for some reason, I felt excited. Now I'd said goodbye to my friends, I could concentrate on the next chapter of my life and start preparing myself for university.

I raised the subject with my landlady over breakfast. I'd told her a while ago that I was moving on, but from the way she went about things as usual, I got the impression that she'd forgotten or at least put it right to the back of her mind. I finished my toast, wiped my mouth with the serviette and waited until she was close enough for me to smell her perfume. For some reason, I wanted to delay it for as long as possible.

"I just wanted to say thank you," I said, fearing she'd be offended and start panicking about the drop in money coming in. To my relief, she just smiled and said, "You're welcome."

The train to Leeds was jampacked with people, but luckily, I'd booked a couple of months in advance. Once I'd crammed my suitcase atop a pile at the end of the carriage, I fought my way along the aisle to my seat. I was relieved, to say the least, to find the reservation tab on my vacant seat.

Things soon evened themselves out, and after an hour or so, the carriage was relatively quiet, with one or two spare seats. That's when I felt able to relax for the first time since breakfast. It's a fair distance from Wiltshire to West Yorkshire. Being quite a small country, the four-hour journey covers most of the country.

Watching the countryside rolling by through the window, I started to get a sense for the first time of how diverse England is and how different it is from the landscape back home in Iraq. Mesmerised by the passing scenery, I stretched my legs and thought back over the events of the previous couple of years. I concluded that I'd become a completely different person as a result of my experiences.

For one, I'd gotten used to having to take full responsibility for my decisions. I had no parents or siblings on hand to offer their advice. Strangely though, I felt closer to them, because for the first time I really missed them as people and not just for the security and comfort they provided.

Then I got to thinking about my time in Swindon. Once, our entire cohort went on a college trip to Torquay, which turned out to be one of those days that stick with you for many years to come. I found myself smiling at the memories of that day and tried to recollect the whereabouts of the many photos I took.

Everyone had acknowledged the winter of 1963 to be the coldest they had experienced, so imagined how I'd felt, coming from a warm country. It's safe to say that I spent a lot of time shivering over my books and I don't know what would have happened if my landlady hadn't kept the fire continually stoked up. From then on, real, open, fires would always remind me of my time in Swindon, as well as my landlady.

And then there was Christmas. Before I went to the UK, I had no idea what a big deal it was for everyone if it snowed over Christmas. There was some snow on the day itself, but the following day, Boxing Day, it started for real. In fact, it didn't stop snowing from the 26th right the way through until the 29th and 30th, when a further 6 inches fell. There was a thick blanket of snow everywhere, whitewashing over the entire landscape, but, as I said before, my landlady made things much more bearable for me.

The freeze had carried on throughout the entire month of January 1963, getting down as low as-16. We'd had it easy though, because in some parts of the country it got even colder, about -20. But -16 was severe enough for them to shut down college for a while. I thought back to how I'd helped out with clearing the snow and ice from the front gate of my landlady's house. I got the flu at one point, but my landlady came to the rescue, bringing me a cup of hot chocolate on a night time, just before I went to bed.

So, with all that reminiscing, the four-hour journey passed by much quicker than I'd expected. I stepped off the train at Leeds station in September 1964 and immediately rubbed my shoulders. I was much further north now and felt apprehensive about how I'd cope with the winter months.

As I was walking through the station, trying to find my way to the taxi rank, I noticed something else, something I hadn't been expecting at all. The people in Leeds sounded much different from the people in Swindon. The accent, it seemed, was just as diverse as the countryside that I'd observed on the train.

The taxi driver sounded so gruff that, by the time I'd reached campus, I was starting to worry that I'd never understand a word anyone said, but much to my relief, the people I met on campus spoke in the fashion that I'd become accustomed to.

The first thing I noticed was the sheer size of the place. I was expecting it to be big, bigger than Swindon and the schools I'd gone to back home, but I wasn't prepared for anything of this magnitude.

I tried to get my bearings through what seemed like thousands of people rushing around, a good few of them looking as lost as I felt. It was 3 pm when I first joined the enrolment queue. By the time I'd got to the front, it was past 5 pm.

The woman, a lecturer with long red hair and glasses, told me to sit down while she found my details. At this point, I was worried that she'd say there'd been some kind of mistake and I'd be sent back home, but she found everything to be in order, so began taking my particulars - my home and term-time address, my next of kin, my preferred method of payment, things like that. After a whole load of talking and signing page after page of see-through yellow paper, I got to my feet and headed for the door. Now I'd enrolled, I had to find somewhere to live as a matter of urgency.

Given the sheer size of the university and the number of new students, I wasn't expecting it to be easy to find decent accommodation. However, it didn't take me all that long. So, after I'd got settled in and unpacked a few things, I found myself at a bit of a loose end, so headed back to campus.

I decided to make the most of my time and have a wander around the department. I met a few of my lecturers, who were surprised to see a new student, wandering around, looking sheepish. Still, they were very friendly and gave me lots of useful information, including the whereabouts of the library.

It was the biggest library I'd ever seen at that point, with thousands of books on every subject imaginable. I asked a librarian that I saw wheeling a trolley full of books to direct me to the science section, where I might find some of the books on my reading list. Following her directions, I made my way to the top floor.

I took a few books from the shelf and sat at a desk, reading them for what felt like hours. Eventually, the woman I'd seen earlier told me that once I'd enrolled, I could take books out if I wanted. So I scooped up the books from my table and took them downstairs to the checkout desk.

Despite the weight of the books, taking them out had given me confidence and a curiosity to explore. I'd discovered all I needed to know to get by at the university, and now it was time for a more significant challenge.

At first, I found Leeds city centre to be somewhat daunting, with all the people, traffic and a multitude of shops. But once I'd found a café that I liked, I gained further confidence, so I set off on my own tour and managed to find places that would be useful, such as book shops and a stationer's that was used to the requirements of university students. The fact that the shop assistant asked me if I was a new student before I'd got a word in, made me feel part of the scene right away.

I started the new term full of optimism and I was quietly confident that I could at least hold my own. But there was a lot of work to get through, and it took some time to adapt. For the first time in my life, a few elements of self-doubt crept in.

I've never been one to shirk a challenge though, and I honestly believe that it was this, coupled with my work ethic that got me through that first term. When I started to struggle, I put in more hours, stayed behind in the library and asked the lecturers for more information. It was those extra hours in the library, when I discovered new and exciting things, that made all the difference, and by Christmas time I was starting to turn things around. I'd advise any struggling student to do the same; go into the library and read, read, read until you find something that makes sense of everything.

In the end, I passed my exams with flying colours and I was happy to begin with, but then, when everyone had let their hair down and got into a party spirit, people started talking about going home. I didn't pay much attention at first, but then it hit me that virtually everyone was going. I was going to be on my own over the festive period and this time, there'd be no landlady to keep me company.

One thing I noticed was that everyone was short of money and kept talking about finding some part-time work to pay the bills. So I decided to use my loneliness to my advantage and earn some cash over the holidays.

I knew Royal Mail would need help with all the Christmas cards they had to deliver, so I used my initiative and went to the post office. I was given a uniform and everything else I needed, such as a list of addresses etc. and began my new part-time job.

I have to admit that it was hard work, much harder than I'd expected. The sack was heavy and having to trudge through the snow didn't make things any easier. There was a strong sense of camaraderie among the postmen, which was most evident in the canteen that I visited once my daily rounds were completed. I was glad to wrap my hands around a hot mug and feel the sensation of hot liquid in innards, warming me from the inside out.

The early mornings aside, I enjoyed this job and I even felt a bit sad when the time came to start preparing for the new term. But, as I already knew, leaving people behind and moving on is just a part of life.

When the new term started, I soon found that my preparations had put me at a distinct advantage. This was because I already had a thorough understanding of the subjects, so I could tackle the more advanced topics more easily and quickly than everyone else in the cohort.

By the time the Easter holidays came around, I was well into my stride and I knew how to turn my loneliness into an advantage during the holidays. I soon found another job, this time at Wimpey in the town centre

I made good money at Wimpey, enough to see me through the Easter semester without having any kind of financial pressure. This freed up more time for my studies. I was more than happy with the results I attained at the end of the first year, but there was room for improvement, so I spent the summer thinking of ways to better myself.

If the first year of a degree is all about becoming familiar with the subject, the second year is when you really get down to business and learn the things that you expected to learn. I knew this and so prepared myself by getting as far down the reading list as I could before the Autumn semester began.

I soon found that all my preparations had been a worthwhile endeavour. I was enjoying every second of every lecture and learning new things all the time. I was getting a long way ahead and starting to think about what I was going to do after my degree. Then I went home one day to find a letter on my doormat. It was from the Iraq National Student Union, UK & Northern Ireland branch. They were inviting me to be their representative in the European Student Union meetings.

I had no hesitation in taking them up on the offer and for a while, I was on the crest of a wave. Then I started to feel it was eating up a lot of my self-study time, at which point it became a burden. So, I reluctantly passed on the honour to someone with a bit more time on their hands.

The spring semester came and went in an instant and I entered the exam room brimming with confidence. I still felt the same way afterwards, as I'd seen nothing on the papers to make me think I'd attained anything other than top marks. I was feeling relaxed about my results and starting to think about the critical final year, when I got another letter. This time it was from the consulate of Egypt, inviting me to visit the country during the summer. Great, I thought, at last I'd have the opportunity to go home and visit my family.

I boarded the plane and realised, for the first time, that I wasn't the only one to have received an invitation. We got talking, and then it transpired that the invitations had come directly from President Nassir himself.

When we landed in Cairo, we were all as surprised as each other to find a senior official waiting for us at the airport. He took us straight to a 5-star Hilton hotel, which we were delighted and surprised to find was overlooking the Nile. During the short transit ride from the airport to the hotel, the change in temperature became increasingly noticeable. I'd been in England, a mostly cold country, and now I was in one of the hottest places in the world. I worried about how I was going to acclimatise to the heat and if I'd be able to do it again when I arrived back to the UK.

It wasn't just the weather that was different. The way people dressed, their mannerisms, the way they greeted each other; all that felt alien yet at the same time familiar.

At the end of the visit, we gathered in a hotel dining room and waited for a senior official to arrive to give a speech.

The speech was stirring, to say the least. In fact, I'd even go so far as to say that he was one of the most exceptional speakers I've ever encountered.

To be precise, it was a long speech, in which he said that we (the guests) would build an industrial country that would go from strength to strength in the future. His words resonated with me and proved to be an inspiration throughout my studies and beyond.

During the flight home, I kept thinking about the speech and why it had been so impactful. From everyone's faces, I got a sense that it was because we were all so young and ambitious. We could do anything to develop the country as Nassir had predicted.

It was only once I got a job several years later that I realised that the country couldn't grow so long as it was led by a dictator. So I suppose it was this stay in Egypt that would shape my views and my destiny for my life after university.

Bodington Hall of residence was to be my home for my final year of study. It was 4 miles north of the main campus and within walking distance of the main ring road where I caught a bus. I found the services at Bodington to be first-class and, better still, there was a reading library, which I used over and over to do my course work and to revise in peace.

I made the decision at the start of my final year (66/67) that I was going to go all out to attain the very best grades that I could. I had decided to go on to further academic study, and I wanted to make sure that I had enough UCAS points to be accepted wherever I chose to go.

During lectures, I took as many summarised notes as I could. Then afterwards, when everyone else was making their way back home, I used to stay for a while in the library and rewrite them. That way, if I needed clarification or if I had any ideas that sparked my imagination, I was in the best place to carry out all the research I needed to. The library was usually busy, and I'd have to walk around for a while to find a relatively private place to sit. Still, occasionally, later on after an evening lecture, it would be quiet and I'd have more or less an entire floor to myself.

Sometimes even the library didn't satisfy my appetite for knowledge, so I'd have to make an appointment with the lecturer, who gave me the answers to any discrepancy I'd been unable to solve for myself.

I wouldn't say my final exams were easy, but when I put down my pen and scraped back my chair for the last time, I felt reasonably confident that I'd achieved my goal of improving on the grades I'd attained for the second year.

We went for a night out to mark the end of our exams. While everyone was fretting over their results and worrying about their future, I was able to remain calm. Looking at the nervousness etched across their faces, I felt glad that I'd put in the extra work, which had enabled me to relax and savour the moment.

When everyone went home to see their families after the exams, I felt a bit regretful that I couldn't see mine, but again, I turned a bad situation into a positive one, by finding a temporary job in Sheffield, just until the results were formally declared.

On the day itself, I travelled to Leeds and for the first time felt the nerves. There was always the possibility that I'd been overconfident and I'd misunderstood something.

I felt relief more than anything when I found out I'd passed. Then when I discovered I'd achieved the highest honour possible, I filled up with pride. At that point, all I wanted to do was tell my family that I now had a degree in electrical and electronic engineering, issued by one of the top universities in the UK.

Shorty after my graduation, I had a decision to make. I received a letter from the University of Birmingham and then another, a few days later, from the University of Alberta, in Canada. They were both offering me scholarships to study for a higher degree.

This was great news, but it got better still. Because my grades had been so good, they both considered my degree to be the equivalent of a masters', so were letting me go straight on to a PhD.

Whilst the offer of a scholarship from Alberta was tempting, I'd done all of my studies in the UK and for all I knew, the education system in Canada might not be quite up to standard. So it was for this reason that I decided to remain in the UK and, consequently, I chose Birmingham.

My designee supervisor had managed to get some scholarships from the Research Council and offered to fund my PhD, which, as you can image, made me a very happy man.

Then, when I was just about to register at Birmingham, I received a letter from my supervisor, saying that he was moving on. He was going to be the new head of department of Electrical and Electronic Engineering (which was my subject), at the University of Bradford and he could no longer fund my PhD. Things worked out OK for me though, because he said he could transfer the funding, providing I moved to

Bradford. I replied immediately, congratulating him on his success and saying I'd like to accept his kind offer.

At Bradford, I found myself to be a member of one of the first cohorts of students to study for a PhD at the new red brick university.

I arrived at Bradford in October 1967. I'd applied for a place at one of the university's halls of residence more out of hope than expectation, and I was surprised and pleased when I was successful. So, by the time I came to enrol, I'd already settled in and made one or two friends. It also meant that I could concentrate on my studies right from the off, without having the distraction of having to worry about where I was going to live.

After enrolling, as it had stood me in such good stead last time, I went to look around the department and to meet some of the lecturers. I found everything to be awe-inspiring and the library too was as big, if not bigger then Leeds. Leaving the building to head into town, I got a sense that I'd made the right decision. Not only was I going to enjoy every minute of my studies, but I was going to attain my PhD with top grades, although I knew that because I'd skipped the intermediary masters, that it was going to be a massive jump from a degree.

I was surprised to find that one of my best friends was studying in the same department as me, so we spent a lot of time catching up whenever we had a break, which made me feel even more comfortable in my new surroundings.

As I was walking through the city centre, the cold wind cut through me like never before during my stay in the UK. However, I went to a restaurant, and to my surprise discovered they served a lot of Asian cuisines. The food was slightly less expensive than it had been at Leeds, which was and still is good news for a full-time student.

There is a big Asian community in Bradford, which welcomed me with open arms. After spending three years away from home, being with these people and talking about subjects we were all familiar with put me right at home.

I much enjoyed my initial appointment with the supervisor. He was very approachable and told me about the project requirements without being asked. He also suggested I use the department's laboratory to carry out my work, which made me eager to make a start.

I left his office feeling so excited that instead of going back to the halls, I went straight to the library to find some articles on the topics that my supervisor had spoken about. That was when I first discovered that very little had been written about advanced technology. This meant things were going to be a bit harder, but also opened the door for me to become an authority.

I knew from my prior experiences that being prepared for this exciting new challenge was paramount. I only had funding for three years so, as the majority of PhDs took four years at that time, I had to collate information as I went along during years one and two. This meant staying in the laboratory long after 10 pm and going to bed more or less straight away when I arrived back at the halls, as I had to be up bright and early the following day.

Prior to the final year of my studies, I left the halls of residence to make way for new students and so found myself living in rented accommodation in the city.

As I'd done much of the research already, I felt confident that I would complete my thesis on time, so I began modelling the results when everyone else was starting from scratch.

It was at this time, partly because I was so far ahead, that I became aware of the need to relax some. Consequently, I began meeting up with colleagues after hours and attending some social events. It was at one of these events that I met my future wife.

She was working at a primary school in Bradford and lived in Baildon, a small town near Shipley, with her parents and two brothers.

There was an Indian restaurant in Shipley that quickly became one of our favourite places to go out. We'd go there, or to a Greek restaurant in Baildon that we also liked, in her white mini. In summer, we ate fish and chips or ice cream if it was really hot. It didn't take us long to realise we had much in common and form a bond that I suspected might be unbreakable for many years to come. So, with my PhD out of the way, I took the plunge and asked her father if I could have his daughter's hand in marriage. I was aged 24 at the time.

I found her father sat in front of a roaring coal fire in the living room of her house. I felt nervous, and a bit intimidated to start with, but once I'd found a chair near the fire, I began to relax. As soon as he opened his mouth, however, the nerves returned and I was conscious of this as I replied to his questions.

First, he asked me where I came from and about my degree, which I felt more than comfortable about telling him. I'd done really well with my academic studies, so I knew he was going to be impressed, and impressed he was. Then I asked him about the marriage and for a few seconds, he looked into the fire while he gave the matter some thought. All I could hear was the crackling fire and the rest of the family going about their business in another part of the house. Then, without warning, he looked me in the eye and said we were too young.

Then it was my turn to look into the fire, attempting to hide my despondency, which surely must have been written all over my face.

"But," he said with an air of authority, "In the end, it's my daughter's decision and if she agrees, who am I to stand in her way?"

I can't remember my emotions ever going from the depths of despair to elation in such a short space of time. I thanked him and left the room to find my future wife, trying to think of the best way of popping the question.

All four of us went out for a meal that night, for what felt to me like a celebration. My wife looked bemused at my high spirits, and partway through the meal, I think it dawned on her, and she became as elated as me.

She accepted my proposal without hesitation, giving me the wholly pleasurable task of booking a time to register the marriage at the mosque and contacting my best friend to make sure he could act as a witness.

All official documents had to be endorsed by the marriage office back in Iraq, giving us time to think about arrangements and make the necessary preparations. In the end, we decided that she should continue working at the school and finish the academic year, while I go home to Iraq and find a place for us to live. A year later, she moved over to Iraq to join me

Chapter 3:

I bent down to pick up the letter from the brown, horsehair doormat. Continuing on my way, I turned it over two or three times to try and determine who it was from and if it was good or bad news. When I saw the university's stamp, I had a fair idea of what it was about, but I couldn't be sure.

The letter fell through my fingers and landed on my lap. It was confirmation of my graduation, along with an invitation to the graduation ceremony in July 1971. The ceremony was to be held in the presence of Harold Wilson, who was the honorary chancellor of Bradford University at that time.

As tempting as it was, I didn't attend the graduation ceremony. I'd spent eight years away from home and had been looking forward reuniting with meeting my family. Attending my graduation would mean I had to spend a further six months in the UK, so I decided not to, despite the presence of Harold Wilson.

There was another reason I wanted to go home. They knew nothing of my impending marriage and, while I was confident they'd be happy for me, I was feeling a bit nervous about telling them, for a reason I couldn't quite put my finger on. Delaying for a further six months would only prolong my apprehension, and there might also be unforeseen implications for my marriage. So, I bought my return tickets, which were an element of my funding contract, and started preparing to go home.

On the plane, I found myself sandwiched between a middle-aged man with a big belly and a grey suit, and a well to do looking woman who spoke to the flight attendants like she was the

Queen. I wasn't in the mood for socialising, so once they'd finished with the food and drinks (which the man slurped), I had a lot of time to think.

I couldn't be sure how my family would react to me marrying an English woman. They wouldn't have been expecting this when I left home. So, I gave a lot of thought to how I was going to break the news. I couldn't be sure of when would be the right time, so I decided to wait until I arrived home. If I couldn't plan in advance, I'd just have to take the opportunity as it arose. I put my hand in my pocket and rubbed the ring between my thumb and forefinger. It would have to stay where it was until I'd made my announcement.

As soon as I saw my parents and siblings waiting for me at the airport, I dropped my bags and ran towards them. It was one of the most joyous moments of my life, and seeing them made it hit home how much I'd missed them. I hugged my parents until I worried about crushing their ribs, and then I moved on to my siblings.

We had a short catch up in the car, but it wasn't until we arrived home and we'd had some food in our bellies that I got to find out what everyone had been up to while I'd been away. All my siblings had changed a lot. My older brothers had grown into men, but the most significant and noticeable change had occurred to my brother, Hussein. He was 17 now and a man himself in all but the law.

The nine-year-old boy that I'd left behind had gone forever. I'd missed his transformation into adulthood, all his ups and downs that had inevitably occurred along the way. Tears welled in my eyes as I thought about how my absence might have impacted him. Did the other siblings give him as much help and guidance as I would have? They surely must, but that was little consolation for missing out on his adolescence

I pulled him aside later, and we sat chatting alone, just us two for a few minutes. I told him how I'd missed everyone, but him especially, and how I felt about missing his adolescence. We both got a bit choked up. When I felt a tear roll down my cheek, I decided it was time for us to go back and revel in the company of the rest of my family.

I slept soundly that night. All the time I'd been away, I never considered myself to be a light sleeper, but I must have been, because that night I slept better than I had for years. I slept so well and so long, that I was still feeling slightly sleepy when I woke up. Then, not long after I'd eaten, my mum informed me that I had a new uncle, who was waiting to see me in the living room.

This made me feel excited, intrigued, but at the same time a little wary. Anyone would be suspicious of a previously unknown relative and anyway, what if we didn't get on or we had views that were miles apart?

I needn't have worried though, because the second our eyes met, I knew we were going to be good friends. He shook my hand a little too tightly and gestured at the seat nearest to him, where he could get a good look at me. I was a bit curious about where he'd come from, but didn't want to risk spoiling the jovial atmosphere that was in every corner of the room.

When my mother left the room once, I was within a whisker of confiding in him about my marriage, as I had been with Hussein the night before. Fortunately, I managed to keep my lips sealed long enough for the moment to pass.

For the next week or so, it seemed all I did was meet new relatives and catch up with those I knew well. I was having such a good time that it would have been easy to forget about the salient subject, which was starting to weigh a bit heavy. It's wasn't that I was afraid of telling them, it's just that if they disapproved it would spoil the atmosphere, which I wished could have continued forever. However, I knew that couldn't possibly happen.

Once things had settled a bit, my mum asked me if I wanted to accompany her on a visit to her two elderly sisters, who lived six hours' drive away, in Basra. As I had some spare time on my hands, and because I hadn't seen them for a long time, I agreed to go with her. It was only once we were in the car, listening to the roar of the engine and watching the countryside rush towards us through the windscreen, that I realised the perfect opportunity had arisen. If I didn't tell her now, and such an opportunity didn't arise again, I'd only have myself to blame.

I waited until roughly five hours had passed, then I asked the driver to pull over at a layby. My mother looked at me with a puzzled expression, and I informed her that I had something important to say that couldn't wait until we got back home. "OK then," she said, as the indicator started to tick.

Waiting for the engine to cut out and for her to give me her full attention, I said, "Mum, I have something to tell you. I'm err—engaged."

The shock was written all over her face. "Engaged? Who to?"

"A woman I met in England. An—English woman." I held my breath as I recalled broaching the subject with her father.

"Mosa, that's OK, I don't care if she's English. Just as long as you're happy."

I let out a long sigh of relief. "But what about—"

43

"Your father will say exactly the same thing as me. And if he doesn't, he'll have me to answer to."

I smiled for the first time that day.

"Is that why you've been so quiet, Mosa? Have you been worrying yourself about telling me?"

I nodded. "You and Dad."

I enjoyed seeing my aunts even more for getting the news of my marriage out in the open, and found myself living in the clouds for a while, just as I had when she'd first said yes. It wasn't until the journey back home that my thoughts turned to Dad. But, as I had Mum onside, I couldn't see that I had much to worry about.

My dad was overjoyed at the news, saying that I was just at the right age to be getting married. I explained that I had to find somewhere to live, to which he replied that he'd do all he could to help me, and that I was welcome to stay there until I found the perfect house.

With all the catching-up over with, and the news of my marriage out in the open, I could progress to the next item on my agenda, which was finding a job.

After a short search, I contacted the grant authority, who asked to see my papers. They kept me waiting for a few days and then offered me a job. I cannot overemphasise how elated this made me feel. I wanted to shout it from the rooftops that all my studying had been rewarded. Most of all, I wanted to tell my wife, so I felt a bit frustrated that I couldn't.

My job was with the National Radio and TV Broadcasting Authority, which was in the Salhia district of Karkh. I was responsible for overseeing future projects.

The Director-General of the authority, Sa' aid Al-Sahaf was a humble and amicable man. I'd only met him a few times before it became apparent that we were going to get on well. He even said I could work or hold meetings in his office.

I had no difficulty in motivating myself to get out of bed on a morning. I couldn't wait to get to work, and people noticed my enthusiasm right from the off. In my absence, national radio broadcasting had fallen by the wayside, so my first project was to oversee its upgrading.

The minister for Information at the time was Tariq Aziz, a decidedly patriotic man. He was adamant that Iraq should be able to broadcast its voice to the wider world. It didn't take long for Iraq's radio to be up and running again, less than a year in fact.

Not long after I'd started working for the National Radio and TV Broadcasting Authority, I arrived home to find my mother holding a letter, which turned out to be from my wife. She wanted to spend Easter with me in Baghdad, so she could get to know my family and see for herself everything I'd described to her. The two weeks she stayed will always hold a special place in my heart.

First of all, I took her to Habbaniya tourist village, which has a beach and a vast lake. It is a resort in central Iraq that is very popular with tourists. We spent several days walking along the beach, watching everyone swimming and generally having a great time.

My family took to her right away and welcomed her as if she was already a family member. This pleased me much, as my wife and my family was the centre of my life, and now I could see them both together. Just before she left, she said she would relocate at the end of August 1971, to avoid the blistering hot summer months.

As soon as she'd settled in, we went flat searching. We found a flat near my family home, in an upmarket area of Al-Adhamiyah. We thought we'd be very happy there, and it was the perfect place to start a family, so we informed the landlord that we'd like to rent the flat and moved in soon afterwards. I was earning a modest salary at the time, so we bought basic furniture, without any frills, but we had our own place, which was the most important thing.

We decided to join Baghdad social club, where we made lots of new friends. We used to attend as often as we could. It was frequented by lots of ordinary people, but also some well-known figures such as politicians, artists and poets etc. It was an opportunity to become acquainted with people that could do us a lot of good, although this was by no means our motivation for going.

The club was a great place to socialise all year round, but it was especially enjoyable at Christmas. Aside from the chatter and festive mood, there was a coal fire which kept us all warm and provided a cosy atmosphere for everyone in attendance.

All the upheaval hadn't affected my work in the slightest, and I was enjoying it as much as ever. In addition to the radio, I also oversaw several other exciting projects, which included the development of regional TV stations and the Education TV channel. All these projects were completed while I was employed by the Radio Broadcasting Authority. However, after a year, I felt it was time for a new challenge.

In 1972, the government of Al-baker established a National electronic Research Centre, the purpose of which was to provide technical support to public services and government departments. They chose me to be the centre's director, by a presidential decree.

It took me just a year to build an advanced research laboratory, an achievement which made me and my family incredibly proud. We also considered many other exciting projects including designing an advanced encryption algorithm for senior officials' telephones; a surveillance system to scan for hostile radio transmissions; the provision of x-ray equipment to scan the incoming and outgoing goods at airports, plus antijamming systems and more.

Having recently completed a PhD, I had no hesitation in making the laboratory available to postgraduate research students.

It was in 1972 that my wife became a teacher at the Monsour private primary school. That summer, we left the private rented accommodation we'd lived in for the past year and relocated to a single room in my brother's house. This was because my wife was pregnant.

One day in April 1973, I stepped outside and paused to let the cool breeze wash over my face. The sky was blue, and the sun was mid-way between the Eastern horizon and the highest point in the sky. It was warm, but not too warm. It was the kind of day that made me feel ten feet tall, and for this reason, I decided to walk to work. The weather aside, it was just a typical day, but when I arrived home, everything had changed forever.

My wife had gone into labour. Whilst I'd been at work she'd gone into labour, relying on the rest of the household to take care of her.

I raced to the Al Haidary maternity Unit, of Street 52, Karrada, where I was relieved to find my wife in good health. This was partly because everyone had gathered to help her. I was glad people had been willing to step in for me, but I felt a bit guilty, nonetheless. Out of desperation, she'd called on an old school friend, who, like her, was a Yorkshire lass. She was still with my wife when I arrived, stood over the bed, talking sympathetically to her. As she had a good knowledge of the local dialogue, my wife had asked her to act as interpreter.

A couple of hours after I'd arrived at Al Haidary maternity unit, my wife gave birth to a baby girl. Our first child had been born.

Chapter 4

Three months after the birth of our first child, something happened that I would never forget. I arrived in my office, for what I thought was a routine day. The wind blew in through the open window, ruffling some papers on my desk, as I tried to complete a document I'd started the night before. I had a glass of water to hand and I could hear people walking about and talking loudly in another part of the building. Like any other day, I found this distracting.

Somewhere in the distance, a car approached, but I had learnt to block out background noise when I was trying to concentrate, so let it go over my head. When it became evident that it was heading for the building in which I worked, I heard excited chatter coming from another office. It turned into the car park outside, and everyone went deathly quiet. It was some time before anyone spoke, and when they did, they sounded worried, afraid even. I gave up and put down my pen

There was a knock on my door. I got up to see all what the fuss was about. As I opened the door, my colleague was just about to talk when the doors to the main entrance opened, and we heard unfriendly voices. When the door shut and footsteps ascended the bottom flight of stairs, we knew. My colleague looked over his shoulder as the steps got closer. Foreboding was written all over his face. Then the soldiers reached the top of the staircase and marched towards us.

They came to a halt about two metres away from us and cocked their rifles. Then one of them stepped forwards and barked, "Dr Abu-Rgheff? Which one of you is Dr Abu-Rgheff?

We fell silent for a second, until one of my colleagues insisted that we'd never heard that name before.

Five rifles clicked into place and pointed in our faces. "I'll ask you again. Which one of you is Dr Abu-Rgheff?

I stepped forward. "I am."

The soldiers tied a blindfold around me and pushed me forwards towards the stairs. I stumbled on the first stair and would have fallen, had one of the soldiers not grabbed me and thrown me sideways, smashing my back against the wooden bannister.

They urged me forwards, pushing me in the back as I descended the stairs with caution.

Once outside the building, the door behind me slammed shut, and they marched me towards what sounded like a jeep with the engine rumbling. I heard voices, which grew louder with each step forwards, and then someone jumped out and opened the back door. I was thrust onto the back seat, where I was sandwiched between two soldiers. They were determined to give me a rough ride to wherever it was they were taking me.

I protested my innocence and tried to get some answers as the car rolled over yet another divot in the road.

The humidity in the car, which had all its windows wound up, made perspiration pour down me, soaking my blindfold and making my lips taste salty. I tried every other minute to run my hand across my forehead, but was prevented the second I moved my arm towards my face. By the time we reached our destination, I could feel the patch where the sweat had dripped onto my work trousers.

The car screed to a halt and the door opened. A gust of warm, dusty air engulfed my face, drying the sweat and cooling me down. My relief was short-lived though, because I soon felt what I guessed to be the barrel of a rifle poke into my back. "Move it," the soldier barked. I put one foot in front of the other, placing all my trust in my captors and wondering what would happen if I accidentally strayed.

A door swung open, catching my toes. I was again shoved in the back, causing me to trip over the doorstep and fall tumbling to the cold, hard floor.

I heard a different voice, a woman, say something to them, which I couldn't quite catch. They pulled me up off the floor and led me along a corridor. Although I was still blindfolded, I could tell that the passage was getting darker with each step I took. Eventually, they stopped close to what I sensed was the end of the corridor and took out a key. Seconds later, there was a click and a heavy door opened towards me.

"Get in." I stumbled forward, but this time just about managed to stay on my feet. The next thing I knew, a few of them had entered, leaving the door open. They marched towards the back of the cell, where I sat with my back to the wall.

"Up," one of them, the nearest of them barked at me.

I struggled to my feet, but apparently not fast enough. The same soldier that had shouted at me seconds earlier grabbed the back of my collar and hauled me up. Then he pushed me forwards, slamming my ribcage against the damp, concrete wall. I couldn't help but wheeze every time I breathed in.

The next thing I knew, the soldier was binding my arms together at the wrist. The rope cut in tight, leaving no room to move. I feared my blood circulation might be cut off.

He raised my arms until my wrist came into contact with a small metal object on the wall. It didn't take me long to work it out what it was. He pulled my arms up until I felt a pain in my shoulders and then lowered them, forcing what felt like a hook into the tiny gap between my wrists and the rope. I was in agony. They must have walked across the cell to the door, but I was in too much pain to notice. All I heard was the door banging shut. The keys chinked, the locked clicked and they walked away, laughing and joking.

I held my breath as the footsteps receded. Eventually, they reached a door, which, I could tell, was just as heavy as the door of my own cell. When it banged shut, all I could hear was the sound of my own breathing.

I moved my wrists to try and loosen the rope, but I only succeeded in making it tighter. I kicked out against the wall, and then took a deep breath to curb my frustration. I turned to face the wall, to give my predicament's a moment's thought. For a while, all I could hear was my own breathing again until, somewhere along the corridor, I heard something. As hard as I tried, I couldn't hear a thing above the all-consuming silence.

I was left like that, arms bound up above my head, my shoulders burning and my wrists blistered, and tingling due to a reduced blood supply.

In an attempt to pass the time and forget about the pain, I cast my mind back to the events of the last few weeks.

Two weeks previously, on 30th June 1973, President Ahmed Hassan al Bakr (AHB) was due to arrive back in Iraq following an official visit to Poland and Bulgaria. At first, everything appeared to be proceeding as usual, until it was noticed that some important officials were missing from the welcoming party. Nadhim Kzar

Dr Mosa Abu Rgheff

Director of Internal State Security (Secret Police) and two ministers were highly conspicuous in their absence.

While AHB was in mid-air, roughly two hours before he was due to land, there was an attempted coup.

Kzar and his supporters seized Lieut. Gen. Hammid Shihab, the Defence Minister, and Lieut. Gen. Sadoun Ghiadan, who was the Interior Minister. They were held at gunpoint and then thrown into the back of a van and taken away. Kzar and his supporters took them towards the Iranian border, which is roughly 110 miles to the east of Baghdad.

The military dispatched helicopters to watch the roads, but it was dark and foggy, so they didn't find a convoy of automobiles until the morning. Baathist militia were quick to cut them off.

During the encounter that followed, General Shihab was killed and General Ghaidan wounded. As for Kzar, he was captured unhurt.

Kzar and his supporters were tried, but the trial was headed by Izzat Ibrahim A̲l-Duri, who was a member of the ruling Revolutionary Command Council. The outcome was, therefore, a foregone conclusion. After the guilty verdict was read out, they were bound and taken away.

The following day, it was announced on Baghdad radio that 23 people had been arrested and executed following their failed attempt to overthrow the government. When I was working for the National Radio and TV Broadcasting Authority, I couldn't possibly have foreseen that my endeavours would be used for this purpose.

Kazar had a crucial role in the police force. He was director of the national public security department. This gave him a considerable say in the country's internal affairs. However, he was not as important as the 15 member council, which formed the inner circle of power.

The council's Vice President, a man called Saddam Hussein, broadcast a statement shortly afterwards. He said that Kzar's clique had been limited to the public security department and that it lacked support from the armed forces of the ruling Baath party.

The pain in his arms was unbearable. He clenched his teeth and focused his thoughts on his theory as to why the coup d' ètat took place to begin with.

After spending a few minutes contemplating, during which the agony faded into background, he concluded that everything must have centred around AHB's absence. It was the perfect opportunity for his deputy, Saddam Hussein to try and usurp him. He'd probably been plotting it for months and in hindsight, the clues were there.

It was a commonly known fact that AHB suffered from diabetes. Therefore, there was a good chance that he was ill, maybe even during his absence. Hussein would have been one of the few people to know this.

Mosa fell into deep thought for a moment, before concluding that his motivation, at least in part, could have been to halt Khomeini, who was planning to export his revolution to Iran's neighbouring states. Hussein knew he was a serious threat that had to be stopped before it was too late.

It was just a theory, but an interesting and quite likely theory nonetheless. As this was based on the facts he currently knew, his theory could change when he was released and his wife updated him.

The noise, the one, I thought I'd heard earlier, drifted along the corridor once more. I strained to listen and, despite my pain, managed to make out that I was not alone. This knowledge gave me a crumb of comfort, but it quickly dissipated when I heard the door open, and footsteps proceeded along the corridor towards

When the footsteps bypassed my cell, I felt relieved in one way and frustrated in another. If the guard hadn't come to see me, it meant that there was no news and my agony would be prolonged.

Some time later, the atmosphere changed. Everything became quieter, somewhat calmer, and the chatter from the guards and other

Dr Mosa Abu Rgheff

captives ceased. This, I assumed, was how it was at night. I submitted myself to my heavy eyelids and hoped that I would pass out during the night to alleviate the pain for a few hours at least.

Chapter 5

Things were worse at night. To begin with, there wasn't much difference, all I could think about was the pain, but then as each hour passed, my body told me it was time to sleep.

There was an occasional noise outside, a dog barking or the distant rumble of a car engine and somewhere along the corridor, some guards were talking, laughing, making jokes.

At one point, I guessed at around 3 or 4 am, I held my breath to try and listen for noises coming from other cells. I wasn't on my own, I knew that, but as they were so quiet, maybe they hadn't been subjected to such cruel treatment. Or maybe they were beyond thinking.

Just as my eyelids started to flicker, a ray of light, only a tiny one, came in from somewhere. Then there were voices. I listened carefully to what was going on. When I recognised one of the voices as belonging to the guard I'd encountered the day before, I assumed the night shift was ending. My second day in detention had begun.

I heard movements in the other cells, which offered up the opportunity to find my bearings. I'd just managed to work out that I was roughly halfway along the row when the sound of heavy footsteps emerged. He, I assumed it was a guard, ran his fingers across the bars of each cell he passed, until he came to me. This time he paused, and for a moment I thought he was going to produce a bunch of jangling keys, but he just grinned at me and moved along, running his fingers over the bars and sometimes giving them a shake too. I guessed this was to unsettle the cell's occupants and plant a fear that today might be their worse yet.

That's when I first felt the pangs of hunger. I hadn't realised until that moment that I hadn't eaten since the previous day. It was becoming increasingly unlikely, as each minute passed, that they were going to come round and serve up breakfast.

So I was left hanging for what felt like a few hours, my thoughts flitting from my arms to my stomach, until there were more footsteps. The bars of a far off cell, perhaps the one closest to the guard's room rattled. But, unlike earlier, the noise was soon followed by the sound of keys. There was a short exchange before the door closed, and the process repeated at the next cell.

By the time he'd reached the cell that was next door but one, the vicinity was overcome with the most revolting smell. I didn't even attempt to work out what it might be. When he entered the adjacent cell, I could hear for the first time that my neighbour was a young man. Probably well educated, and from the way he kept gasping between his words, there was a high chance that he'd been left with his hands above his head in the same way I had. I wanted to ask him what had happened, and if he could tell me why he was being detained, but I knew that wasn't going to be possible. What I did learn though, was that this was a different guard. He didn't sound anywhere near as hostile as those I'd encountered previously.

"Mosa," he said, knocking on the bars, "Mosa, are you OK? Time to eat."

For a second, I felt like I was in a zoo, but I decided not to dwell on the thought.

I gestured at my arms with my head, and seconds later, he had the key in the lock.

He entered, carrying something on a tray, which, I have to say, looked just as vile as it smelt. Nonetheless, I knew that I'd feel much better for eating it, so didn't protest.

He placed the food on a table, that, from what I could tell, was a couple of feet behind me.

I let out a sigh of relief as my hands dropped to my side, but I hadn't noticed until then how weak I felt at the knees. He lifted me up off the ground and guided me to the table.

I'd just finished chewing my first mouthful, which tasted better than it smelt, when I heard him walking back towards the door.

"Wait," I called, hoping he wouldn't notice how much effort I'd put in, just to speak a single word.

To my amazement, he stopped and turned around. "Yes, what is it?" He took a step towards me.

"Do you know why I've been taken captive?" I asked this, because I had to, but I knew deep down that he would be reluctant.

"Yes, I do, but—I'm afraid I can't tell you."

"OK, I understand."

Later, roughly an hour later, the same guard returned, only this time he had company. As soon as they started talking, I noticed the second person was the guard that had tied me up the day before. It was the food guard that entered though. "Get up!" He barked.

I was surprised by how easily I got to my feet. The food, as bad as it was, must have done me some good.

"Come on. Move it."

Once I was up on my feet, he shoved me against the wall, tied my hands and put the rope through the hook. Without another word, he marched out of the cell and banged the door shut. The lock clicked and they moved on to the cell next to me.

I definitely felt better for having eaten. For a short while, the pain in my arms eased up and I could think more clearly. I'm not sure when it was, probably about two or three o'clock, assuming we had eaten at noon, but the food started repeating on me. I had to fight off the urge to vomit, which took my mind off my arms for a while. I reached a point where I could keep it in no longer, and I was sick. From the sound, I could tell that most of it went on the wall, but I did get a smattering on my white work shirt. It dripped between the shirt buttons, creating a hot patch on my chest.

The smell was nauseating, but that wasn't my main concern. Now I'd brought up the food, my stomach was empty, and I felt just as light-headed as I had earlier in the day, if not more so.

So I was left like that, with my arms above my head for the rest of the day. The smell made me retch every now and then, and I felt sure that if there was anything at all to bring up, I would have. The changing of the guards signified the beginning of the night, which were even worse than the days. I was tired and weak, but still couldn't manage to get any sleep at all.

Day 3

No sooner had the day guards arrived, and the distant sound of chatter and arguing ceased, then a guard, perhaps the same one as the day before, began his rounds. And just like the day before, he ran his fingers over the bars. This time though, he tried extra hard to unsettle everyone. Instead of just sneering and walking on, he shouted insults, which someone took exception to. The guard was quick to unlock the door. There followed the kind of noise I thought I'd never hear from a grown man and then—silence.

The guard continued walking along the aisle in the same manner as before, only this time no one retorted.

Passing my cell, he ran his fingers along the bars. Then, laughing to himself, he shook them and moved on. With only the heel of his boot visible, he stopped and looked at me over his shoulder. In addition to the pain in my arms, I was both tired and hungry, plus I could still smell my own vomit from the day before. He took a step backwards and the room filled with his laughter.

He stared through the bars and murmured my name. I twisted my neck to give him what he wanted. He gestured with his finger for me to move towards him, so I leant forwards as much as I could.

He raised his chin, pressed his forehead against the bars, pursed his lips and spat at me. It landed in the centre of my forehead, equidistance between my eyes, and crept downwards along the bridge of my nose.

"Take that, traitor," he shouted, before moving on.

Although he continued to disconcert each of the prisoners as he walked along the aisle, I couldn't hear him shout or play the same trick that he had on me on anyone else. From this, I gathered that I must be a special case.

The spittle had stuck to the inside of my blindfold, which in turn made the blindfold stick to my nose. It was uncomfortable to open my eyes fully so I spent a while squinting, trying to listen to what was going on outside, at the same time as imagining how my cell might look from the information I'd gleaned so far.

At what I assumed to be the same time as the day before, the smell of food drifted in my direction. For some reason, it didn't smell anywhere near as disgusting this time. Even though there was a dry patch of sick on the floor directly beneath me and my shirt was still stained, I found myself in a state of eager anticipation.

Hearing the lock click and the doors open, looked across my shoulder, not knowing what to expect from him. He came in, carrying a plate of food and addressed me with the same friendly manner as he had to begin with the day before.

He put the plate on the table and unhooked me. "How are you, Mosa?"

"I'm fairing up well, thanks."

"I see the food didn't agree with you yesterday. You'll get used to it."

He led me to the table. This time I was able to lift the fork to my mouth. I began chewing, tentatively at first, but once I'd swallowed, I couldn't eat it fast enough. The plate was already half-empty when the door creaked open.

"Wait," I called.

His footsteps approached me. "What is it?"

"Can you give me any idea as to why I'm being detained, anything at all?"

"I'm afraid not. Look, if you want my advice, you 'll stop asking questions. Detainees that keep their heads down and don't make a fuss are treated a bit more leniently when it comes to... "

"When it comes to what?"

"Oh, nothing. I've said too much already."

As my head had cleared somewhat, and I'd adjusted to my new surroundings overnight, I was able to judge the time-lapse between feeding time and the second visit. I concluded that it couldn't be any more than ten minutes. That made sense, because they were unlikely to give us enough time to muster up strength.

On his return, the guard had undergone a complete transformation. Just as he had the day before. He shouted at me to get on my feet, yanked my arms high above my head and put me back on the hook. He left the cell, muttering. Then he said something I couldn't quite catch to the other guard, the one that spat at me, and they continued clearing up.

Because the knot was freshly tied, it had lost the give that had built up over the previous twenty-four hours, so it cut tighter than it had before. I was left alone to cope with the monotony and the pain in my arms for the rest of the day, and the night that followed. After the third night, I still hadn't managed to sleep at all.

Day 4

By the fourth day, I was starting to become accustomed to the routine. The chattering guards signified the end of the night shift, the guard came round, then there was a break for what felt like hours until the food arrived. That was now my favourite part of the day; the part that I looked forward to all night and, to be honest, kept me from falling off the edge.

I ate the same vile food as before, was re-hooked and then resigned myself to the agonising monotony. It was identical in every way to the day before, until the locked clicked and someone stepped inside.

"Time to answer some questions," he barked at me.

I was relieved to hear this. Not just because it would divert my thoughts away from the agony in my arms for a few minutes, but also because by giving answers, I might get some answers in return.

He approached me, his heavy breathing filling the room, drowning out the sound of his footsteps.

"Name?" he shouted.

"Mosa— Dr Abu-Rgheff."

"Address?"

I gave him my address. He went on; place of work, marital status, no. of children—even my qualifications and my place of study.

I heard him fold up a piece of paper and shove it in his pocket. "That will be all—for now."

I didn't like the way he said *for now*.

"Oh, just one more thing, before I go."

"What?"

"I've been instructed to remove some of your possessions."

"Possessions? But I don't have anything on me."

He threw me to the floor, which I could feel was made of concrete.

"Your shoes."

I gave them to him without protest. They served little purpose, after all.

"And your belt."

I removed my belt and handed it to him. When he asked for my tie, I stood up and took a step forward to steady myself. In my stockinged feet, I could tell the concrete was rippled, with one or two pieces of gravel added for good measure. Whoever had laid the floor hadn't cared much about aesthetics.

I pretended to fall against the wall so that I could touch it, just as I had with the floor. I wasn't all that surprised to find it was made of concrete, but unlike the floor it was smooth, and it felt damp. Most likely the roof leaked when it rained and the water dripped down the walls.

"OK, Abu-Rgheff, time to get you back in position."

He pushed me against the hard, smooth wall, raised my arms above my head and forced the rope over the hook, leaving me with a dull pain in my wrist. It was only once he'd gone that I realised I was going to have to find a way of keeping my trousers up around my waist without using my hands. One thing was for sure; once I got out, I was going to be much more resourceful than I was when I came in. My hearing too, had sharpened. Not only could I hear the guards laughing and joking in a room at the end of the corridor, but I could also pick up a few words of what they were saying.

It was that night, my fourth in captivity, that I finally got a few hours of sleep. If sleep is the correct word. I'd become accustomed to the pain, which was probably why my arms had started to feel numb at the shoulders. I contemplated if and how the pain would return after I'd been released for a few minutes so I could eat. Maybe they released me just so they could play mind games, with the intention of reinforcing the pain

I believe doze is the word that is used in normal circumstances. Doze—it's a soft word that is often used in the same sentence as an old man or a baby. No one would ever say it in prison. Intermittent sleep is preferable.

So I slept intermittently, waking up when the guards got rowdy to listened in on their conversation. At one point during the night, there was a big argument and threats were made. Soon after, I got a tickle in my throat and despite my efforts, just couldn't stop myself from coughing.

Almost immediately, the guards started muttering to each other, and angry footsteps approached. I hung my head and shut my eyes. The steps came to a halt outside my cell and a bright light, probably a torch, shone in, making me squint under my blindfold.

The lock clicked and the door swung open. He stood next to me and jabbed at my side. "How much did you hear?" he shouted in my ear.

"Nothing, I replied," which, on this occasion, was the truth.

"You're lying."

He jabbed my side again, in precisely the same place as before, and with more venom. "I said, how much did you hear?"

"Nothing. I've been fast asleep."

78

To my amazement, he took a step back. "Oh, well as long as you keep that attitude."

The door slammed shut and he marched back along the aisle.

I found myself falling into a dizzy, dreamy state, and my eyes closed. I slept for what I guessed to be an hour or so, until I was awoken by more shouting and laughing. I listened to the noises coming from outside the building; the distant rumble of cars, dogs barking, rubbish rattling around in the breeze. I then drifted off again, roughly half an hour before the guards changed over, and my sixth day began.

I have to be honest and say nothing much happened for the next few days. I slept intermittently at night, was released for a few minutes to eat and then was left with my arms above my head for the rest of the day. I soon discovered that the guards spoke about the same trivial things all the time, so even that was of little interest to me. I did, however, spend a lot of time trying to form a complete picture of my cell. The walls were not made of concrete as I'd first thought, but plaster, which in part explained why I could hear noises coming from other cells along the row.

I was confident that if I had the right tools and the know-how, I'd be able to break through the wall quite easily. But I didn't have the tools, so there was no point in following that particular train of thought. Not that I'm the kind of person that would try to escape anyway. I decided to take the lunchtime guard's advice and keep my head down, but this made me wonder exactly what he had meant when he said they'd be more lenient on me.

After replaying the conversation in my head several times, I concluded that they had something in store for me, something that I wouldn't enjoy one bit.

Chapter 6

Day 9

The guard walked along the centre aisle, rattling the bars and shouting insults just like any other day. By this time, I'd blended in, and I wasn't receiving any special treatment. So he became insignificant, like a holster to a pistol.

A few hours later, the guard appeared with my food as usual. He unhooked me, moved me sideways to avoid the puddle of blood that had dripped down from my arms, and sat me at a table to eat.

I gobbled the food down. Like so many things, I'd become accustomed, so I was able to appreciate its sustenance. I now wished there was a bit more of it.

The guard walked away. I was expecting to hear the door shut and his trolley rattle onwards when he asked me, extremely cautiously, if I would like to have a walk around my cell for a few minutes.

I jumped at the chance. I sensed he was stood at the door as I stumbled my way around the room, running my fingertips over anything within reach. Most things were just as I'd imagined – concrete floor and bare plaster walls, but the bars—they were made of timber, not the metal that I 'd wrongly assumed.

Although it was just a small thing, the revelation uplifted my spirits immeasurably.

When the second guard appeared a few minutes later, there followed a heated exchange. The new guard, the one that hooked me to the wall every day, was angry with the first.

The altercation seemed to end quite amicably though, so I didn't think much of it. I spent the rest of the day enjoying the revelation that had added some detail to my mental image of the cell.

I spent most of my time thinking about my friends and family that night, more than usual. I couldn't believe that I wanted to tell them about what I'd discovered as much as I did; I wasn't quite sure why this was so. I then lost myself in my thoughts. My wife was a strong woman. She'd be coping better than most. When eventually I did get some sleep, it was of better quality than usual. I only woke twice as I recall, when the guards got a bit rowdy, and a joke went too far.

Day ten started like any other.

Day 10

I listened carefully to the guard as he ran his fingers across the bars and gave them a rattle. I'd been waiting for this moment for the last twenty hours or so. The clues had been there all along. The way his fingers hit the bars didn't ring out as does metal, and I could tell it was wood when he knocked on them with what sounded like his knuckles. I couldn't believe how stupid I'd been to think they were made of metal. It felt like I'd scored a small victory, the first since I'd been taken and wondered what this might lead to.

After what I guessed to be four hours of trying to work out what my family might be doing, I began to feel hungry. Sure enough, the smell soon started to drift along the corridor.

I first noticed something was wrong when he was roughly midway between myself and the door. He sounded a bit more gruff than usual. I smiled to myself as I wondered what might have put him in such a bad mood.

Then he stopped outside my cell. I did my best to turn round and greet him with a smile, but as I did so, he shouted through the bars to keep still.

I heard him take a plate from the trolley and the bad smell got even worse, as it always did when he put the food out. Next thing I knew, he was inside and the door banged shut.

It was only once he'd unhooked me and shoved me towards the table that I knew.

"What's happened to the usual guard?" I said, trying not to sound as weak as I felt.

"He's been relieved of his duties."

"Why?"

"Oh, let's just say, he had a run-in with the boss."

He went quiet and moved up close, until I could feel his breath on my face. For a moment, I thought he was going to spit at me again, but instead he just laughed and left the cell.

Day 11

With my arms above my head, as they had been since I arrived, I was thinking about my family and how they were coping. I was sure they would cope without me, as they were strong. But they'd be worried sick nonetheless, and for that, I felt terrible. Still, my distress was occupying a sizable chunk of my thoughts, which was helping the time pass a bit quicker.

I could hear the guards changing along the corridor, signifying the start of the night hours. I had no idea what time this took place every day, but the atmosphere did turn right away. I felt like every sound I made was being scrutinised, and one step out of line would have severe consequences.

My thoughts returned to my family. Just as I was about to settle for the night, the door at the end of the corridor burst open. Angry footsteps approached. As they grew louder, I sensed that they were heading my way. And I was right.

My cell door swung open. "OK, Abu-Rgheff, your moment of reckoning has arrived." He unhooked my arms, held them behind my back and nudged me forward. The floor turned smooth as I left my cell for the first time in days.

It wasn't a long journey, no more than a couple of minutes, but in that time, I discovered a lot about my prison. When I heard voices, some of them spitting out insults in my face, I knew I was passing through the room where the guards congregated at night. Then there was a sharp turn, and I felt a soft carpet underfoot. It felt like heaven.

Another sharp turn and the floor froze over. It was straight ahead from then on, until I was ordered to halt. From over my shoulder, the guard opened a door and pushed me into a room with no light.

The guard greeted another man with much respect, before throwing me down on a chair. He retreated to somewhere behind me, probably by the door. After giving the guard some instructions, a man started talking. He was sat in a chair directly opposite me, that much I could tell.

He fired questions at me, one after the other. I knew the answer to pretty much all of them and couldn't see any reason not to be open with him.

Roughly halfway through the interrogation, the way he said a specific word sounded vaguely familiar. From that moment on, I concentrated on trying to identify him.

It was Taha Al-jezrawi, who was a senior minister in the regime.

When the questions stopped, he ordered the guard to take me back to my cell. However, knowing this was the best chance I'd had to get answers to my own questions, and that I might not get a better opportunity, I called for the guard to wait. Al Jezrawi told him to do as I'd asked.

I took a deep breath and asked him why I was there. I sat there in silence for ten seconds or so while he gave it some consideration.

When he spoke, it was only to tell me that this was something I didn't need to know.

I'd heard this man, the interior minister, talk a lot so I knew when he was in two minds about something. As the door was still ajar, I decided to persist. I told him that I'd been taken without explanation and held for two weeks. I said I'd told him all he wanted to know, adding that it was only fair that he answered my question in return.

While my persistence paid off, his tone immediately turned hostile. "Those who are educated in the west make trouble for us." He instructed the guard to take me back to my cell.

I walked with my head held high, feeling better than I had since I was taken. He pushed me into the cell, tied me up and slammed the door on the way out. When he re-joined the other guards, I heard him recounting the interrogation. I got the impression that they wanted some retaliation for my minor victory, but it was a price worth paying. I spent the rest of the night trying to piece together the jigsaw of why I'd been taken. I'd been identified as a possible trouble maker, and now I was determined to learn why I'd been singled out.

Days 12-18

By the time morning came around, my high spirits had dissipated. When I thought about my wife and daughter, and the trouble I'd made for them, my minor victory felt insignificant. Indeed, I even felt selfish for feeling happy while they were at home, most likely worrying themselves to death.

I started thinking about hypothetical scenarios, that had little chance of coming true. It helped me pass the time though, as there was nothing at all to relieve me of the monotony.

89

I stared in front of me at the divot on the grey wall, which was starting to make me feel nauseous. My wife at home. She'd be taking our daughter to my parents now, or maybe she'd already done that and was now arriving at work. That was if she was still working in my absence. I hoped she was. I didn't want anyone's life to be put on hold while I was away. And even more than that, I didn't want them to be hanging around the house fretting over me, although I knew they probably were.

My arms.

My daughter, who had only been born three months before. Was she missing me? Would she recognise me? What about if I never got out or I was sentenced to death and she had to spend her life without a father? How would that affect her? Would she turn out just the same as she would if I was there to oversee her transition into adulthood? Probably not. But maybe she would if my wife remarried. I couldn't quite comprehend that. This would have to wait for another day, when I wasn't hurting so much.

I'd had a happy marriage. The time when I went to ask her father if I could marry her. I was terrified, and for a moment I thought he was going to say no. But he didn't, he said yes, and I'll always be grateful to him for that. It probably brought us closer together in the end. A shared experience that we could laugh about when there was nothing else to say.

The strings that joined my arms to my shoulders slackened, taking my pain to a whole new level.

My mum and dad were sat at home worrying about me, just as hey had been for every minute of every day since I was taken. My wife probably went round to tell them or maybe she phoned?

When I get out, sunshine will shine on my face. The breeze might be cool, it might be hot or there might not be any breeze at all. My wife and everyone else will be there waiting for me. I wonder what they'll be wearing, and if my dad will be with them. But maybe they don't know where I am, and I'll have to find my own way home.

When I get home, I'll finally have some proper food and this food I 'd become accustomed to will make me feel sick each time I think about it. I'll go to my parents and my mum will cook something special.

My arms . . .

Day 19

Shortly after the nightshift commenced, a door banged and footsteps approached.

I listened to each of the individual footsteps, noting the timing between each. This is the kind of skill you pick up when you've been locked up and blindfolded for weeks.

They grew louder and louder. Then, when they were at their loudest, they started to slow. I waited for the sound of jangling keys.

"OK, Abu-Rgheff," the guard said, rattling a key into the lock, "your presence has been requested."

As soon as he spoke, I knew it was the guard that had had it in for me since I was first taken. True to form, he released me from the wall and threw me to the floor. I placed my hands on the rippling, cold concrete and pushed myself to my feet.

Taking my hands, he pushed his knee into the small of my back and shouted at me to walk forwards, then, as the floor turned smooth, he ordered me to turn right. I kept on walking, entirely at his mercy.

Just like the previous week, I passed through the guard's room, where, also like the previous week, I was subjected to a barrage of insults. For some reason, they kept on using the word 'traitor' in some shape or form. I just brushed this off, like it was nothing. When my feet touched the carpeted area, I knew exactly where I was going, and the feeling of vulnerability left me.

As he opened the door, I got the feeling eyes were on me, only this time there was more than one pair. The guard released his grip and removed my blindfold.

A bright light shone into my face, causing me to squint and look down to the floor. I spent about 30 seconds rubbing my eyes with some

93

vigour until I looked up, expecting to see who it was that was watching me with such interest. To my surprise, the guard and I were alone.

He nudged me forwards and ordered me to walk up and down.

Each time one foot landed in front of the other, I imagined I was about to trip up. Despite the removal of my blindfold, I was still off-balance. It was highly likely that they found me comical. I was so desperate for the ordeal to be over that I picked up the pace in an attempt to make it a brief humiliation

"Slowly!" the guard shouted.

When the floor ran out, I turned to retrace my footsteps and stumbled. I steadied myself and continued walking back and forth in the dark until I heard another voice shout out.

The guard walked across the room to talk to whoever it was that had called out. After a short exchange, in which the man whose face I hadn't seen clearly had the upper hand, he turned around and told me I could stop. He put the blindfold back in place, allowing a bit more slack than there had been before.

Back in my cell, the guard tied me and left me without saying a word. Waiting for his footsteps to leave the vicinity, I reflected on the strange occurrence I'd just participated in. Many theories passed through my mind and then, after what felt like hours, I formed a conclusion. It was highly likely that the person watching in the darkened room was Lieut. Gen. Sadoun Ghiadan, the interior minister that was injured in the coup d'état. If I was correct, it was probable that the interrogation team had asked him to identify the perpetrator. I'd just taken part in an identity parade.

I didn't know if I had been identified incorrectly or not, but either way, my newly acquired sixth sense told me that my stay in this detention camp was about to come to an end.

From that moment on, the guards, even the one that had spat at me, treated me with a modicum of respect. The food seemed to taste better too. They did tie me to the wall just as before, but now there was a lot more room for manoeuvre, meaning the blisters could, at long last, start to heal.

It came as no surprise then, when three days after the parade, a guard burst into my, cell waving some documents.

"Dr Abu-Rgheff," he said, almost politely, "You are free to leave."

He helped me down from the wall, removed the rope from my wrists and threw it into a corner. Next, he reached behind my head and removed my blindfold. For the first time since I was taken, I was able to get a look at my cell.

The bars were indeed made of solid, polished timber. The walls were plaster, just as I'd imagined and the floor looked like someone had taken a spade and thrown concrete around at random. Everything was just as I'd pictured it in my mind's eye, until I looked at the wall that I'd been facing. The divot that I'd come across not long after I was first tied, the one that had kept me going like a trusty old friend, was tiny and insignificant.

The guard called for me to hurry, once again addressing me by the title I'd worked so hard to attain. I staggered across the cold, hard floor for the very last time.

Chapter 7

They took me beyond a heavy, wooden door and into a corridor that I knew I'd never been down before. From then on, we turned this way and that until a ray of sunshine came in through a window. This was the first time I'd seen or felt the light of day for three weeks and it felt like a highly significant moment. At one time, a week or so earlier, I had thought that I might never feel this sensation again. Whatever happened from this moment on, I knew I'd never take sunlight for granted again.

The minute I stepped outside, they pushed me forward, grunted in my ear and left me to fend for myself. After I'd taken a moment to bask in the sunshine and let a tepid breeze wash over my face, I addressed the matter in hand. I couldn't wait to go home and see my family, but the trouble was, I had no way of getting there.

I had the idea of flagging down a taxi, but as I had no money, I'd have to get lucky and find a driver that was sympathetic to my cause, who would agree to let me pay once I got home.

In 1973, few drivers were willing to do this. The sunlight was starting to fade by the time I finally found the right driver.

I climbed in, made myself comfortable and watched the road ahead move towards me over the driver's shoulder. I tried not to think about the journey there, but I just couldn't help it. I felt a shudder go right through me. That was when I realised that it was going to be one of those experiences that people don't forget in a hurry. I worried that it might weigh heavy for some years to come.

When the indicator started ticking at the corner of the street, the bright sunlight returned, and it felt like I was floating in mid-air. In just a few seconds I'd be holding my wife and kissing my daughter. I was about to step right back into heaven.

I got out of the cab and walked along the path as the taxi's engine rumbled on. I saw my wife and daughter through the window, and my mother too. They looked forlorn indeed, and maybe even a bit pale. Probably they'd had even less sleep than me over the past few weeks. At least I'd had my thoughts of them to keep me comfort, all they had was worry.

I looked back over my shoulder at the watching taxi driver and then back through the window at my family. This wasn't going to be as easy as I'd thought. I stood outside for a few moments as I tried to devise a plan.

Somehow, I would have to go inside and find some money, postponing all the outpouring of emotion that was about to take place.

So, I tentatively inched open the door with the intention of finding some money without alerting them to my presence. But, just as I'd expected, my efforts were in vain.

My mother opened the door and was about to fling her arms around me when I held a finger to my lips and asked her to shush. I whispered to her that I needed some money for the taxi, which she handed to me. Two minutes or so later, the driver was on his way, and I was opening the door again. This time it was for real.

My wife didn't notice when I first stepped into the room. My mother was stood behind me. I could feel her smiling at my back, using my newly acquired six sense.

My wife was staring through the window, my daughter in her arms. She looked utterly lost in her thoughts and, knowing they were probably about me, I felt guilty for what I'd put her through.

My mother coughed to gain her attention.

"Mosa!" Her scream was so loud, people at the end of the street could have heard. She carefully put our daughter in the crib before getting to her feet and running across the room with her arms wide open. This moment, which I'd thought might never happen, was one of the most joyous of my life.

Once we'd let go of each other, my wife smiled down at our daughter, who was fast asleep in her crib. She looked so peaceful, completely oblivious to what was going on around her. My wife lifted her and handed her to me, doing her best not to wake her.

I couldn't help myself, though. I lowered my head, kissed her forehead and then held her up to eye level. I hugged her as tightly as I dared, kissed her again, and passed her back to my wife, who looked as happy as I'd ever seen her.

We spent a while sitting there, catching up and generally enjoying ourselves. Then there was a fatal break in the conversation. The joy turned into relief, and one or two tears were shed by everyone.

We sat in silent contemplation for a while, my wife periodically checking on our sleeping daughter. Eventually, my mother wiped her eyes and said we should go out the following day, all of us as a family. My wife and I thought this was a brilliant idea, and the joviality returned.

From that moment on, everyone stopped crying, and we spent the rest of the night talking about our extended family and joking about things that had happened in the past. When my mother said that my dad would be getting worried about her, I took her home in the car.

The following day, we went out as planned. We visited the park, browsed some shops and generally had a great day. And then, to cap it all off, my dad took us for a meal.

At first, everyone continued in the same high spirits that we'd had all day. Then the waitress came to clear the plates, and there was a moment's silence. I recalled how this led to a sombre atmosphere the night before and readied myself.

This time, it was my dad that asked me where I'd been and what had happened. My mother told him to let it go and to give my wife and I chance to talk first.

We went home for a while, until my dad said it was time for them to go. Then, just as they were leaving, my mother told my wife that she'd watch her granddaughter the next day, to give us a chance to talk.

We took our daughter to my parents' at around lunchtime and returned home to a quiet and empty house. It had only been a few weeks since our daughter's birth, but already, the house felt strange without her. I made myself comfortable on the couch.

"So, are you going to tell me what happened?" My wife said, leaning forwards.

I gave her a summary of events, from the moment I was taken, to the second I was released and had to hail a taxi to take me home. I spared her the details for her for fear of upsetting her and causing her more distress than I had already.

When there was a break in the conversation, I asked her how she had coped and what she had been up to. I thought I knew what she was going to say. I expected her to say that they'd been worried sick, and she hadn't been able to concentrate on her work. I thought she was going to tell me that my mother had been just as worried, if not more so. She did all this, but once she had finished, there was more to come.

She took a deep breath, shook her head and told me she had some news that I wasn't going to like.

This came as a big surprise to me. I couldn't imagine what she was going to say. Maybe it concerned our daughter or my mother. I could never have predicted what followed.

Sometime during my absence, there had been a clamour to seize every one that was thought to have been a traitor. Some of the people loyal to AHB had turned up outside our house, shouting at the gates. They were claiming that I was a traitor. My wife hadn't known what to do. She wanted to go outside and tell them to go away, but she was afraid that they might hurt her and our daughter.

I told her she did right to stay inside and not to worry about me.

She wiped her eyes and continued. The insults got louder, the things they were saying worse. A few of the neighbours came out to see what the fuss was all about. She could hear them gossiping in the street, which distracted her. Next thing she knew, the protestors were shaking the door, making it rattle as if it was about to fall off its hinges.

Terrified, she grabbed our daughter, took her upstairs and prayed that one of our neighbours would be gallant and persuade them to leave.

But eventually, the inevitable happened, and they broke in. My wife ran downstairs, still holding the baby and had to watch helplessly as they searched the furniture for evidence. When they left empty-handed, everything in the house had been upturned and ransacked. She said she worked through the night to get it cleared up so that she'd be able to sleep, knowing she wouldn't be reminded the moment she got out of bed.

I couldn't believe what I was hearing, although it made perfect sense. I recalled how, partway through my imprisonment, everyone had started calling me a traitor. Although I didn't say anything to my wife, I guessed that this was when it must have taken place.

I can't describe how I felt about this. It was like they had taken me and gone out of their way to destroy everything I held dear. This led me to believe that I'd been singled out, but from what I could gather, I wasn't the only person to have been taken.

It's fair to say that things felt strange on the morning of my first day back at work. To begin with, I just couldn't stop fretting about my family and even contemplated getting in my car to go home, partway through the morning. I'd just about decided on this course of action when there was a knock on my door and a colleague, one that had been present when I was taken, stepped inside.

He was overjoyed to see me. He said everyone had been worried, but they knew I was brave and therefore could withstand everything they threw at me.

He went to fetch us a drink so we could have a proper catch up about work matters. When he returned, he was part of a crowd of people.

Everyone told me they'd missed me and said that I was brave. After this, I didn't really feel like going home anymore. I was still worried about my family, but I decided my wife would insist I turn around and go back to work.

For a few days, it was like I'd been dropped back into my old life where I'd left off. One day, after about a week, a colleague came to see me. He revealed that, according to his sources, I'd been detained in the palace of the last king, which was being used as an intelligence office.

He also confirmed that my parade had been observed by the senior member of the regime that was injured. He'd been there to try and identify the perpetrator. I had been the prime suspect.

I didn't feel the desire to go back to work for some weeks after this. I just couldn't bear the thought of leaving my family and forcing them to fend for themselves should I be arrested again. I kept my ear to the ground and asked people in the know if there had been any more arrests. They told me consistently that, as far as they knew, the seizures had stopped. In the end, it was my wife that persuaded me it was time to go back.

Once everything had settled down, we began to feel our accommodation was a bit cramped.

We decided it was no place to raise a child, so in the Autumn of 1973, we moved for a second time.

Our new home was a two-bedroom apartment in the Karrada district of the city centre. Shortly after moving in, we noticed the area was popular with people of our age. Many had bought land to build a house and to provide a safe place for their children to play. So, we decided to follow suit and purchased a plot, about 1500 meters square. It was located in a northern district of the city called Sha 'b. I got a mortgage from the estate's bank, and we sold half of the plot so that the task of building our house could commence in 1974.

We enjoyed visiting the house regularly to see how things had progressed. Once we could see the house was nearing completion, we felt a tinge of excitement, and we began making plans.

In 1975, when the school that she worked at shut down, my wife found new employment with the UN National Centre. The centre occupied a row of old terraced houses in Street 52, Karrada.

We didn't have far to travel to register our child with a nursery. It was just around the corner from our apartment, which put my wife's mind at rest quite a lot.

In 1976, we went to visit our house, and my wife remarked how close it looked to completion. A few days later, we received notification from the construction company, and it was with a great deal of pride that we stepped inside our house to take a look round. It didn't take long for us to make the necessary plans, what and who was going where, that type of thing.

On the way home, we called in to see my parents at my family home. They were thrilled that we were going to be living just five minutes away and said they'd be making frequent visits. We could tell from their faces that we'd made them very happy. And what made me extra pleased was that my wife was just as happy as I was to be living so close to them. We were going to be one big family. I thought back to my days in the UK when I'd dreamt about this moment and sometimes doubted it would ever come.

As we were both working, no one was at home to look after our daughter, so we asked my sister if she'd take care of her. She readily agreed.

We left our daughter each morning and collected her at night on our way home from work.

In the spring of 1977, my mother in law came to visit. She stayed with us for four weeks in total. I must admit that I hadn't really spent that much time with her before, so I was unable to form an opinion about her. However, I was delighted to find that she was just as charming and warm as my wife. We had a great time while she was there. We took her to see Cteifiphon Arch, which is located in Salman Pak, just South of Baghdad. We also went to the Habaniya tourist village, where I'd gone with my wife when she first came to visit in 1971. It brought back many happy memories for my wife and I. We couldn't let her go home without also visiting the historical sites in Babylon city. It was a wholly enjoyable time for us all, and when she left, I missed her a lot.

Towards the end of 1978, we were told that my wife was pregnant with our second child, which was cause for much celebration.

In the New Year of 1979, my wife's mother invited her to go and visit. I wasn't keen to start with as she would be heavily pregnant, but after much deliberating we (her mother and I) decided it would be safe for her to go.

She boarded the plane to England with our soon to be oldest child, in the summer of 1979. It was hot in England, much warmer than usual. This took my wife by surprise.

My wife's mother made a huge fuss over our daughter, and for a few weeks, they revelled in each other's company. They spent much of the time travelling around, catching up with my wife's family. Then, in early September, my wife went into labour for a second time.

As soon as he'd heard, my brother in law jumped into his car, collected my wife and took her straight to Bradford Royal Maternity Unit. My mother in law got in touch with some of my wife's old friends in Baildon, and they came over straight away, to offer their help if needed. Of course, at any other time, my wife would have been delighted to see them and be keen to spend hours catching up. But due to the circumstances, she just smiled and said hello. Her friends understood.

My mother in law went back home to look after our first daughter, who, unbelievably, was six years old.

I'll never forget how I discovered that I'd just become a father – again. It had been a long day at work so, feeling lonely, I decided to go to bed early and catch up on my sleep. I was just about to change when the phone rang. I walked briskly towards it, part of me wanting to catch it before it rang off and the other part wanting to go to—. It was my mother in law.

She told me she had some news, and I should sit down.

I had an inkling, but I didn't want to assume anything, not till I'd heard the words.

"Mosa, you're the father of another child, another daughter."

I was momentarily lost for words. "Wh— that's wonderful news. How are they doing? Are they OK?"

"Yes, mother and daughter number two are doing fine. However daughter one—"

I felt a lump in my throat. "What about her?"

"Oh, relax. Sorry to have worried you. It's just that she's been crying all day."

"Crying? Why?"

"She woke up, and her mum wasn't around. She's was scared witless and hasn't stopped crying all day."

"But you're her grandma."

"I know that Mosa, but—let's be honest, she doesn't know me that well, does she? It's understandable from that point of view."

"Yes, I suppose you're right. Can I talk to her?"

"Of course. One minute."

There was a pause while she went to fetch my daughter and then, after a muffled conversation, they came back.

I spoke to my daughter for a few minutes, and it quite quickly became apparent that she was feeling much calmer. I asked her to pass the receiver back to my mother in law, who said it seemed to have done the trick.

My wife spent three days in hospital, after which she returned to her mother's house to convalesce. We kept in touch regularly over the phone, and I could tell from the way everyone spoke, that the new baby was a very beautiful child and was perceived as being like a precious jewel. This made me even more eager to meet her, and consequently, I was distracted at work, and the clock took an age to go round.

It was September 1979, when our second child was born. I had to endure two very lonely months before they returned in mid-November. It was one of the proudest moments of my life.

We took our oldest daughter to register at the Muhheje Primary School a couple of weeks after they returned from England, in November 1979. She was a very bright child, and we were confident she'd do well, wherever she went to school, but Muhheje was held in high regard by everyone in the locality, and it pleased us to know we'd secured her a place.

As we were both working full time, we still had the problem of being unable to look after the kids during the day. Once again, my family stepped in to help us. They agreed to have the girls while we were at work. In all honesty, though, they saw it as a pleasure rather than a chore.

We used to wait with our oldest daughter, until she got on the school bus on a morning. Then we'd wave goodbye until the bus turned the corner. We returned home, trying not to think about how much we were going to miss her all day.

On the way back from school, we were unable to meet her, so instead, she went to my family home alone. Once there, she basked in her grandparent's attention and had a thoroughly enjoyable time until my wife and I collected her.

At last, there was time for a social life. At one time, we were members of the University of Baghdad Social Club, which was located in the Mansour district. The club was full of likeminded people, and we met scholars of a similar age to

117

us. The children too forged some long-lasting friendships

We went to the club all the time during the spring/summer/autumn months. We'd often go outside to sit in the garden and watch a film in the fading daylight. We used to stay till late evening when the moon and stars were out in full. Like many things, it was best at Christmas time, when we'd all laugh and joke as we ate Christmas dinner. I remember once taking a long look around me and thinking that I should savour the moment as it might never be as good again.

Looking back, it is clear that the 1970s were the best years of my life and, even though the years since then have also been good to me, I'd give anything to go back and relive them.

Early on in 1980, the government abolished duties on imported cars for scholars like my wife and I. And, as the duty on imported cars had stood at 100% previously, we took the opportunity to buy a small Mercedes. Times had changed, and as a result, we were able to live a little. We now felt safer than we ever had, so we were able to take the family abroad every now and then, without fear of recriminations.

The changes had much more far-reaching consequences. I could attend International research conferences, which gave me the opportunity to network with other researchers. I made a lot of acquaintances and some contacts that might turn out to be helpful.

Each piece of research that got published earnt me in the region of $500. This award did come in handy, although, as a scientist, money is not my main motivation.

Chapter 8

September 1980

September is one of my favourite months of the year. It is a time when the green leaves glisten in the rain and omit a delicious smell. I only wish it could last longer than just a few weeks.

On one such September day, right at the start of the month in 1980, I left work with a smile on my face. Although I enjoyed my work thoroughly, like everyone else, I looked forward to Fridays. As this particular day was the final before the weekend, it put me in high spirits, but the fact that my brother, Hussein was calling in later made it extra special. He'd always popped in regularly, ever since we'd got married, but his Friday night visits had recently become a fixture.

I stopped the car outside my house, opened the door and waited. My family rushed to greet me, as was their way. I lifted my daughters, one in each arm and hugged them, before kissing my wife. I then accompanied them back to the living room, where I heard everyone's news. This was my favourite time of the day. Every day of every week.

"What time's Uncle Hussein coming?" My oldest daughter asked me.

I glanced at the clock on the wall. "He'll be here soon."

My daughter jumped onto the couch to sit beside my wife and started chattering excitedly.

It wasn't long, no more than half an hour, before my younger brother let himself in through the back door and shouted hello to everyone. Usually, he was there waiting for me, but on Friday nights, he attended prayer meetings with a few of his friends. My daughter jumped to her feet and ran to greet him. Whilst I couldn't move quite as fast as her, I wasn't that far behind.

He bent down to scoop up my daughters one at a time. Then, once my daughters had left the scene, we hugged and greeted each other as if we'd been apart for decades. It had only been a week, and that was long enough for everyone.

The second we parted, I told him once again how good it was to see him, and he flickered a smile. Something was wrong.

"What is it?" I asked.

We walked along the passage that took us from the backdoor to the living room, where my family was waiting expectantly.

"Oh, it's nothing. I'll tell you later, OK?"

I nodded. "OK."

My wife and I shifted along the sofa towards the window. Hussein took the seat at he end, as he always did. My daughters were quick to make him feel welcome.

"How's life treating you, Hussein?" My wife asked him.

"Oh, you know. I can't complain."

My wife persisted with her line of questioning. "Well, what about school then? Anything interesting happened this week?"

My brother smiled. He always had interesting stories to tell us about his work life. I could tell they were said for my daughters' benefit, but my wife and I enjoyed them just as much.

Hussein had graduated from university in 1974. He held a degree in science and, consequently, had found employment at a secondary school as a science teacher.

Ever since my return from the UK n in 1971, we'd continued to see a lot of each other. He often used to pop round for a cup of tea, and sometimes his wife came too. When we moved to our own house, the one we'd had built for us, we were no more than five minutes from Hussein's school. We used to see the children pour in and out of school. They walked past our house twice a day, as this formed part of their journey.

My bond with Hussein, who had always been my closest brother, had strengthened even more. It was now safe to say that we were inseparable. He usually came round every night to visit on his way home, but that particular week, he'd been busy with something at school, so hadn't been able to. I'd been looking forward to tonight all week long, and it was evident from the way he was basking in the atmosphere that he had felt precisely the same.

He recounted a tale or two, during which my daughters looked at him with wide eyes, spellbound. When it started approaching the time he usually went home to eat, my wife glanced up at the clock, regretfully. I then recalled what he'd said earlier in the kitchen and asked my wife to give us a minute. She got up and took my daughters with her to sit in the kitchen.

We'd had such a good time that we were still smiling and laughing to ourselves. But as soon as I asked what he had to tell me, the mood turned sombre.

"Oh yes, " he said.

Whatever it was, it was clearly troubling him. He was such a friendly, happy character. Everyone I knew liked him. His sombre expression looked utterly alien.

"Come on, pal, spit it out. You can tell me. It won't go any further, I promise."

Hussein shook his head. "No, it's nothing like that. It's no secret."

"Well, what, then?"

"Mosa—I've been called up. I've been put in reserve."

For the past few months, it had been looking increasingly likely that we were going to war with Iran. Our neighbours had a vast army at their disposal, and if we were going to stand a chance, we couldn't let ourselves be outnumbered.

It's not often that I'm lost for words. Being a scientist, I'm quite stoic by nature. I never let emotions cloud my judgment of anything. But right there and then, there was nothing I could do. felt my eyes start to tingle.

126

"Mosa, my dear brother."

We fell into a hug.

Hearing my wife emerge from the living room, we quickly parted. I didn't want her to see me like this.

"What's going on?" she said, looking at each of us in turn.

"Oh, nothing." I couldn't see any point in prolonging her worry. With what had happened to me, She'd had a lifetime's worth of anxiety already.

Later that night, when our daughters had gone to bed and we were alone, she asked me again. I could tell by her tone of voice that there was no getting out of it this time.

"He's been called up to fight in the war." I turned my head to look at the floor.

"Oh, Mosa, he'll be OK." She leant forward and patted my thigh.

"I hope so. But, we don't know that . . . do we?"

127

Hussein continued to come round each night to visit, but the news had cast a shadow, and things weren't same. Instead of the storytelling and laughing, we now watched the news in silence. By the second week of the month, it was clear that war with Iran was imminent and my brother was going to the front line.

Of course, I missed him very much, we all did, but he was granted leave quite often. He left on 22nd September, and we saw him at least twice before he was given an extended leave for the New Year holidays. He was in high spirits, as happy and friendly as ever. No one in the family could imagine him harming anyone, which in a way made us even more fearful for him.

On the morning of the 7th January 1980, we were awoken by a loud knock. I quickly got dressed and ran down the stairs, cursing whoever it might be for disturbing my sleep. As soon as I opened the door, my frustration turned to concern.

"Mum, what is it?"

When she swallowed before answering, my concern was itself replaced by a foreboding that turned my legs to jelly. "It's Hussein."

Although I knew he was on leave, it didn't stop me from thinking the worst. I just assumed that he'd been recalled at short notice. "Tears flooded onto the floor. I struggled to form any words at all.

"No." I lunged forwards, planted my head into her pectoral and cried until her top squelched.

"No, "she said, patting my head, "Mosa, stop crying. It's not as bad as that."

I stood up straight. I continued to cry, only this time they were tears of relief. "What is it then?"

She looked around before asking, in a murmur, if she could come inside.

Hussein's wife had banged on the door the middle of the night, distraught. This is what she told my mum:

At about 10 PM, a car screeched to a halt outside their house. There were voices, then the thud of a car door closing. They sat in silence for a minute, holding their breath, praying it was a neighbour, and not them that was in trouble.

When footsteps approached, Hussein, who had become fearless since he joined the army, sprung to his feet and assured her that whatever it was, he'd sort it out.

They told him there was a question to answer. He replied that he was home on leave after spending three months fighting for his country. But it made no difference. She ran to the window and managed to catch a glimpse of him wearing a blindfold.

They shoved him into the car and drove off into the night.

As I was still reeling from the assumption I'd made earlier, it took a few seconds for it to register that he was in grave danger. I shuddered at the thought that he might experience what I had eight years previously. Hussein had been away fighting, he had no interest in politics. I couldn't imagine how he could possibly be perceived as a troublemaker.

I went to work each morning in silence, spent the day watching the clock go round and returned home, wondering if there was any news. Something that might lift my spirits and put an end to this nightmare.

Each night I found my mother sat beside my wife, doing her best to comfort her. My first instinct was to ask if there was any news, but Mum always beat me to it. She thought I might have heard something, anything, during the day. I tried to solace her, saying no news is better than bad news, but it made no difference.

Although I was distraught myself, I knew I had to be a good son and stay strong for my mum's sake. Once she'd gone home, it was my wife's turn to be strong for me.

The New Year's celebrations we'd enjoyed as a family were a distant memory by the time Hussein reappeared. It was 28th January, February almost upon us.

Not long after I'd come back from work and slumped into the chair, my dad came in through the back door. "I have someone to see you," he said, poking his head around the living room door, where all my family were gathered. "Wait a minute."

Through the window, we watched him walk back to the car. He opened the passenger door and waited, patiently. A fragile, desolate figure stepped out on to the pavement. My dad stooped to help him to his feet. It was only when he staggered forwards onto the garden path that I recognised him as Hussein.

I ran along the garden path to hug him. For a moment, I was so pleased to see him that his state didn't register. It was only once we'd parted and I took a good look at him that I filled up with a strange combination of sorrow and anger. "Come on, old chap," I said, taking over from my dad, " come inside, let's have a good look at you."

As I led him towards the front door, for some reason I felt compelled to be positive. I had to try and pretend that everything was OK. Once my wife set eyes on him, I couldn't continue with the pretence.

She hugged him, just as I had, trying to hold back the tears. It was such an emotional moment that no one noticed my dad lurking behind us.

In the living room, my daughters ran to greet him, but my wife called them back and told them to sit quietly. They were good children and so did as she asked without protesting.

We sat in the living room for a while, trying to put a positive spin on things. It reminded me a lot of when I'd been released from detention centre eight years previously. Only this time the suffering he'd endured was much more prominent.

The moon's outline was just about visible by the time my dad stood up and said he'd best be getting home to see my mum. The last thing she needed was having to worry about him on top of everything else.

We all agreed that he should do this, so I walked him back to the taxi car. I stood talking to him for a few minutes whilst my dad held the driver's door ajar. He told me to try and find out what had happened, but to tread carefully. I said I'd try, but couldn't promise anything.

My wife went to make some tea and took the girls with her, leaving us alone to talk for a few minutes. I wanted to broach the question, but I knew from experience that he might not be ready. I studied him for a moment or two, then decided it was best to leave it for a while, despite what my dad had said.

My wife returned shortly and handed a mug to Hussein. We watched and waited for him to move the cup upwards in the firm belief that a drink would do him good, perhaps at least put some colour back into his cheeks. We started talking, my wife and I periodically sipping our tea. When we placed our empty mugs on the table, we noticed that Hussein was still holding his mug above his knees. He hadn't touched a drop.

My wife was concerned and asked him if he didn't want his drink. Then he tried to move the cup to his lips, and we knew why he'd been so hesitant. It wasn't that he didn't want the drink, more that it was too painful for him to raise the mug. Even trying made him wince in agony.

My wife took his mug, put it on the table and told him it was alright. I couldn't delay asking him any longer.

"Hussein?"

He turned to look at me. He clearly knew what was coming.

"Yes?"

I couldn't ask him outright. Evidently, a more subtle approach was needed. "Remember when we were kids and you fell into that rivulet?"

He smiled for the first time that day. "Oh, yes."

"Lucky mum was there to rescue you."

We both laughed. We went on, talking about our childhood and the way things changed as we got older. My wife was present in the room, but didn't participate in the conversation. She focused all her efforts on keeping the girls occupied.

He asked me about my studies in the UK, and I recounted the tale for the millionth time. He was relishing the conversation, right up until I spoke about my capture in 1973. Then he clammed up.

Reluctantly, I asked him if his experiences were similar to mine.

He stared into space for a minute and then shook his head without saying a word.

"It's OK, I understand." I was fully expecting this response, but I knew I had to try or else I'd have my parents to answer to.

He then said he'd like to go home to his wife and stood up. Not only was he frail, but he'd also lost a lot of weight. There was something wrong with his shoulders, too. They looked straight, which explained his awkward body movements. He'd obviously been subjected to the same kind of treatment as me, but worse. Much worse. I couldn't understand how we hadn't spotted this earlier and had the insensitivity to offer him a drink.

I helped him along the path to my car. It wasn't far to his house, but I knew I had to try and change the subject back to our childhood as it would please his wife if he was in high spirits.

It was a long time before he could eat. My mum and his wife helped him the most, but we all thought it would help his recovery if he came to visit me as normal. Then it was my turn to feed him and raise a hot mug of tea to his lips. We did our very best, but it was evident that he needed professional help.

I began searching for a physiotherapist who'd had experienced with this type of injury. When I eventually found the right one, I notified Hussein right away, who agreed to go with me.

I assumed the responsibility of taking him. It was difficult at first, seeing him stagger into the treatment room and then emerge looking even worse than when he went in. But the next day and the day after, we could see the benefits of the exercises, and so gradually we noticed an improvement. The day he managed to feed himself, the whole family celebrated.

From then on, he made rapid progress. He'd been granted several weeks leave, but as his departure date approached, we all thought he wasn't quite ready.

Then the thought struck me that the army didn't know he'd suffered these injuries and if we didn't tell them he would be accused of desertion. So, my elder brother and I took him to the army unit. As they could see he was in no fit state to return, they understood and notified his commanding officer. It was on the way home that I decided I had to find out what had happened.

A few days later, I came home from work to find him sitting on the sofa, talking to my wife and playing with the girls. I paused to recall how he had looked that first night when my dad led him in. Although he wasn't fully recovered, he had improved a great deal. He no longer looked half-starved for one thing. The turning point had come when he could feed himself. His arms had improved, but they remained in a bad way.

The most significant improvement was in his overall demeanour. He no longer looked or sounded so frail and the spirit that they took from him had returned. I decided to ask the question and hope for the best.

"Hussein?" I said, making myself comfortable on an armchair, " Hussein, what happened?"

He glanced at the floor, and the room filled up with silence. For a minute, I thought he was just going to clam up, as he did every time I brought up the forbidden subject. But not this time.

"They tied me up and hung me."

I'd worked out this much already, from the clues I'd managed to piece together myself. "Oh, you poor thing. I know exactly what you went through, my dear brother." As soon as I'd finished talking, I realised I didn't know a thing. He'd been detained for the same length of time I had, and my injuries were mainly psychological. It was obvious there was more. "There's something you're not telling me, isn't there?"

Hussein nodded. "They hung me from a working ceiling fan."

Judging by the state of his shoulders, this made perfect sense. I told him I was never going to let anything like that happen again and gave him a huge brotherly hug. It was while we were hugging that I realised he was still only telling me half of the story.

We parted, and I returned to the armchair from whence I came. "Hussein, you did very well in revealing that, but there's more isn't there? There's something you're not telling me."

He glanced at the floor and his vacant expression returned. "Mosa, I'm sorry, but I can't. It's just too painful."

"It's OK, you've done well to tell me as much as you have."

I was very proud of my brother for telling me this; it was a significant breakthrough. I knew there was more though, and I was determined to find out the full story by whatever means necessary.

I waited until one night when he'd told me in advance that he couldn't come to visit. After work, I drove along a nearby street, searching for anyone that I'd seen in his company. It wasn't long before I came across one such person, so I pulled over and wound down the window.

"Excuse me?"

The man turned.

"You know my brother, don't you? His name's Hussein."

"Yes, of course I do."

"He was taken at the start of January. Do you know anything about it, my friend?"

"Yes, I heard about that. I'm sorry, I can't help you, but . . ."

He gave me the names and addresses of a few people that might be able to help. I thanked him and drove off. It was getting late by that time, and my wife would be getting worried. So I decided to go home and continue my quest after work the following night. I told my wife where I'd been and that I'd be late again the next night. She understood and said she'd keep dinner warm for me.

So, the next night I went to the address I'd been given. A man of about Hussein's age

141

appeared at the corner of the street and walked towards the car. I sounded my horn as he passed and wound down the window.

"What do you want?"

"Excuse me, sir. Do you know my brother? He's called Hussein?"

I could tell he was about to confirm that he did, but then decided against it at the very last minute. "What's your name?"

"Mosa."

He appeared to recognise my name. "Sure, I know him. What can I do for you?"

"Do you have a minute?"

He nodded. "Yeah."

I opened the passenger door and told him to get in.

"What can I do for you, Mosa?"

I looked over my shoulder and saw a man heading towards us. "Not here."

I took him out of town to a deserted road, where I pulled up at a layby.

"My brother was taken in January."

"Yeah, I know." He looked solemn.

"Do you know what happened to him? All he'll tell me is that he was hung by his arms to a fan. I get the feeling he's hiding something."

The man nodded. "Yeah, you're right, there is more to it than that. But—I'm not sure I should tell you if Hussein doesn't want you to know."

I pleaded with him and asked how he would feel if it was his younger brother that had been tortured.

"OK, I'll tell you, but it isn't pretty. You'd better brace yourself, OK?"

I nodded.

He described to me a scene that left me in floods of tears. His friend told me that he was tied up to the fan as Hussein had said, but once a day he was let down—and beaten until he couldn't move. There was much more to it than that, but this was all I was able to comprehend.

143

My poor younger brother had suffered far more than I had, and no one had a clue why.

When he'd finished talking, I stared through the windscreen, unable to conjure up any words, or indeed any thoughts.

"I told you it wasn't pretty."

"I know." It then occurred to me that I needed his story corroborating before I could accept it as the truth.

"Do you know anyone else that can confirm this story?"

The man nodded and gave me a list of people that Hussein attended Friday prayers with. I managed to locate everyone on the list over the next few nights, and they all said the same thing. Reluctantly, I had to accept the truth.

On 8th January, 2 days after Hussein was taken, I decided to accept a job I'd been offered at the university. It felt strange, walking into a new building and meeting new people after all this time in my previous post, and I had Hussein's arrest to contend with too. Being new to the job, I was keen to make a good impression, but I knew that I must be distracted and that people might notice. I even considered asking them if I could delay my start date for a few weeks, but decided that I wasn't going to let those loyal to Saddam ruin my ambitions, just to suit theirs. I also knew that Hussein would agree with me wholeheartedly.

The Gulf War was roughly a year old by then, and we kept hearing about casualties, mainly of young people. Everyone I knew suspected that they were playing down the numbers. It would certainly be consistent with their past actions.

Whilst I was dismayed with the losses, I was relieved that no one I knew had lost their lives. Then, not long after I started at the university, I got word that this wasn't the case. When I heard that some of my ex-students had been killed, including some that I knew well, everything was brought much closer to home. I cursed the powers that be for creating a war without giving any thought to our young people, and everyone close to them whose lives would never be the same.

Despite everything, I enjoyed my new job, and I was glad I'd made the change. I continued to help Hussein recover, right up until he was able, physically at least, not only to resume his normal life, but to make up for some of the lost time.

I kept hearing about my ex-students and other young people I knew that had died, which made me just as angry as I was remorseful. As the year was drawing to a close, I started looking forward to the New Year, which I thought would be the start of a much happier phase of my life. I was wrong.

Towards the end of a particularly busy day in October 1981, I was sat at my desk in the faculty administration. I was just going about my business as usual. It had been a long afternoon; my legs had been rooted in the same position since midday. So I stood up to have a short walk around the office and chat with people that were doing the same. Invigorated, I was just about to return to my desk when the receptionist called me over.

I smiled at her and walked across the office, laughing and joking along the way. By the time I'd reached reception, my colleagues were on their way back to their desks, so were unaware of what happened next.

The receptionist pushed an envelope across the desk and whispered that some security officers had asked her to give me this.

At first, I wasn't that concerned, but as I inserted my finger under the flap, a chill froze me to the spot. This had all the characteristics of another attempt to take me captive. I could see the receptionist watching me with a puzzled expression in my periphery. I tore into the envelope, extracted the note and held it up to eye level. My presence was requested in the state security's main office. They wanted me to answer a few questions.

After a quick glance up at the clock, I decided to postpone it until the morning and enjoy one more night with my family.

My wife was home from work, making the evening meal and the girls were sitting quietly doing their homework. By the time bedtime came around, I'd forgotten about the note. Once the lights went out and my wife fell asleep, it returned to the front of my mind.

My wife was working at Baghdad International School at the time. This worked out well for us as it meant that she could take our oldest daughter to school. On this morning, it was decided that she should take me to work too as it was only a minute or so out of her way.

Once our daughter had blended into the playground, I informed my wife of the previous night's events, being careful not to show my anxiety. I did this as I usually entered work through the main entrance, which was quite a walk from the security office, where I asked her to drop me. I could tell from the look on her face that she thought this was strange, but she didn't say anything.

I stepped out of the car, waved goodbye and walked forwards with my eyes affixed to the security office door.

I breezed into the office with a smile, as if I wasn't concerned for my safety at all. I said I'd been asked to report to the security office to answer some questions and even made a joke about it. The officer scowled at me and told me to take a seat.

I sat without moving for about thirty minutes until I heard a car approach and then come to a halt outside the security office door. It parked in pretty much the same place as my wife had that morning. They got out, and the car door thudded angrily. From their footsteps, I could tell there were at least three and from the focused way they approached, without saying a word, I could tell they were military. I'd been right to worry.

They tied me to the chair and wouldn't let me move an inch until darkness had descended and the university was deserted. Then they untied me, leaving me to sleep on the cold, hard floor I lay awake all night, worrying about what was coming after sunrise. All the while, I was being watched by an armed guard, who was hoping I'd give him a reason to pull the trigger.

When I woke up, the guard had fallen asleep on his chair. Through the corner of my eye, I spied a telephone on the desk. I crept towards the desk and dialled my home phone number. It was my sister that answered, as my wife had already left for work. My words were so quiet that she had trouble recognising my voice. I relayed to her what had happened, then told her

149

to remain calm and repeat it to my wife. As it was the day of her wedding, I apologised for not being able to attend and wished her luck. I replaced the receiver and walked back across the floor to resume my position. The guard was stirring.

Chapter 9

"Ok, Abu-Rgheff, your time has come," the guard said, rubbing his eyes.

As he stood up, something compelled me to look over my shoulder at the desk behind me. To my horror, I'd left the phone off the hook. I jumped to my feet and, keeping my eyes affixed on my captor, inched back towards the desk.

He eyed me up suspiciously.

"Come on." I never thought I'd feel relieved to have a gun shoved into the small of my back. He took me across the car park, towards a black car. A guard emerged from the back seat to wait, leaving the door wide open. They shoved me onto the back seat, and I found myself sandwiched between two of them, just as I had been eight years previously.

There were many similarities between that journey and this. The windows were wound up, meaning the body heat of the two men on either side made me perspire profusely. It was, however, different in two crucial ways.

Firstly, I was not blindfolded this time, which meant they were happy for me to see where they were taking me. Secondly, and more importantly, I had prior experience.

The rough treatment, the guns, the roasting hot car and the inevitable cell that they were going to throw me in, it was just an attempt to break me. I knew that as long they thought I could be useful, they weren't going to pull the trigger. This, I thought, put me at a distinct advantage.

After about an hour, I realised why I hadn't been blindfolded. They'd taken me deep into the surrounding countryside, turning this way and that every hundred metres or so. Without a map, I'd never find my way home. I looked through the window at the orange sky and wondered when or indeed if, I'd see another sunset.

It was dark when we arrived at the destination. As far as I could tell, it was some kind of disused administration block. They took me along a tiled corridor and pushed me into what looked like an abandoned storeroom. Once the door banged shut, I reached out and switched the light on. Compared to 1973, I was staying in the lap of luxury. I took a good look round at my cell, concluding that I would soon be on the move again to somewhere wholly more unpleasant.

I sat in a corner, listening to the guards coming and going. They were laughing about something, making no attempt to lower their voices. After what I estimated to be two or three hours, I heard a click and the chatter stopped. I switched off my own light and just as I expected, the entire block was filled with darkness.

I retreated back to the corner, where my hand met with something sticky. I tried to think of what it might be, until something crawled over my hand. It felt like one of those huge hairy spiders, but I knew only too well that darkness exaggerates everything. I pulled my hand up from the floor and identified the sticky substance as being some kind of cleaning fluid. I moved to the opposite corner, where my eyes shut, and my chin dropped onto my chest.

I awoke to the sound of footsteps walking up and down the corridor. I was completely sealed in this time, without any bars to catch a glimpse of the outside world. Although I could hear most things the guards said as they passed, it sounded distant, which told me I was behind quite a hefty door. Perhaps one of those fire doors that people have to heave open.

Just to pass a few minutes, I imagined how it would be if someone tried to escape. If they managed to unhinge the door, they'd have to get past the guards. Then, if they made it out of the building, they'd have no place to go. It was the perfect place to hold someone captive. This might explain why the conditions were better than before; it was the location that drained your hope rather than the prison itself.

Using the light that was coming in through under the door, I stepped around the boxes to the light switch. After rubbing my eyes as they adjusted to the light, I studied my surroundings. On the opposite wall, where I'd felt something sticky, were some stripes of rust. It looked like there had been filing cabinets there at one time. I then tried to work out how and when they were removed. And why this building had fallen out of service. It was a mystery that I was going to solve by the time I was moved on, as I was so obviously going to be.

I couldn't be entirely certain, but I was sure that food was served up much later. By the time it arrived, I was feeling a few rumbles in my stomach, as I hadn't eaten for over 24 hours. It was just as bad as before, but I was in a better state, so managed to hold it down. And I felt much better for it.

The foul taste lingered all through the night, and by the time morning came around, I was as thirsty as I'd ever been. I soon heard heavy footsteps approaching, getting closer and louder until they came to a halt outside the door. The locked clicked and I could hear his breathing. He dumped something on the floor before leaving.

It was a metal container containing a pint or so of stale water. It was nothing like the fresh, cool water that I'd known as a child, but at least it was something. I raised it to my lips, trying not to spill any of the precious liquid that would have to last me for a full 24 hours.

I was on my own again. I wasn't blindfolded like before, but I might as well have been for all I could see. I knew better than to leave the light on as this would serve as a constant reminder that I was there.

Recalling the satisfaction I'd gained from exploring my cell using just my sense of touch, and just to occupy a few minutes, I walked around, running my hand over everything. The wall felt like smooth, bare plaster, much smoother than last time. The floor had a threadbare carpet, that had probably ceased to be fit for purpose years ago. Then I found something surprising that I probably would never have known about if

I hadn't learnt to use my sense of touch. Blended into the wall at the back of the room was another door, locked and bolted. It was all very mysterious.

I switched the light on to find I was right about almost everything. Everything but the carpet, although it was only a minor thing. It was, in fact, a rug. I bent down to take a good look and noticed a patch where hard fibres clung together like a group of friends that were terrified of the light.

I sat in a corner, trying to piece together the clues. I was intrigued, but I didn't want to think about it too much, or else I'd solve the mystery, and then I'd have nothing at all to occupy my thoughts. So I switched to thinking about my family. This time I thought about Hussein. When were kids he once jumped into the rivulet near our house. He would have drowned too if Mum wasn't there to rescue him.

The food arrived much later than it had in 1973 and with much less fuss. The guard opened the door, switched on the light, muttered something about sitting in the darkness and placed a plate of something terrible on the floor. My plate was still half full when the door opened again. This time, there were a few of them, carrying what appeared to be a long table, but was actually a bed.

They placed it directly over the sticky patch, grunted something that could have been an apology and left me to enjoy (if that's the right word) my dinner in peace.

Quite predictably, the bed wasn't really a bed. The minute I sat, the springs flattened without any kind of resistance. I got the feeling it wasn't going to be much better than sleeping on the floor. And I was right. But it was certainly better than trying to sleep with my hands tied and hung on a wall. Compared to that, it was like a five-star hotel.

I counted seven of these meals in total until a guard burst in and gestured for me to follow. He took me down a corridor, turning right three times and then past a desk that looked like it had once been used by a receptionist.

It was broad daylight outside. I walked across the gravelly car park to a waiting car, perhaps the same one that I had come in. Just as I expected, one guard was waiting at the door and another was sat on the back seat. I soon found myself sandwiched between them, inhaling their foul body odour.

This was a long journey. They took me back through town, and onto a busy road. I tried to look through the windows at the passing traffic without moving my head. I wondered if the drivers had any idea at all of my situation. A guard noticed and told me to keep my eyes on the windscreen, through which we could see the traffic moving towards us at speed.

As soon as I got out, I knew that I had come from a makeshift detention centre to something that could have been purpose-built. They pushed me through the heavy wooden doors, towards another door on the left. Above the sound of the guard's rattling keys, I heard voices, lots of them.

The door creaked open and I stepped into yet another corridor. This time it was dark and deserted, a bit like a medi-evil dungeon. There were even one or two puddles on the floor from where the roof had leaked, which made the entire block stink of damp. I half expected to see the bulging eyes of a fat rat, sat staring at me on the path ahead, but fortunately, I was spared that at least.

He took me towards a closed door with a ray of light escaping underneath. There was a man inside, wearing a different uniform to the guards. He was sat at a desk, sifting through a pile of documents. The guard caught his attention, displaying a great deal of respect. Then he departed, leaving me alone with the seated man, who was obviously a high-ranking officer.

He made me stand with my back to the wall, while he studied me from behind his wooden desk. He got straight to the point. He told me that I'd committed a crime against the state and I was being detained until the date of my trial. I asked him when the trial might be, but he just shrugged and said he had no idea. From the way he sniggered, I gathered he was playing mind games, trying his very best to push me towards breaking point. He said that was all and called for the guard.

I counted six cells, three on the left and three on the right. As we walked past the first and then the second, I thought for a minute that they had something else in store for me, until he tugged at my sleeve and told me to halt outside the third cell on the left.

I looked around at everyone, feeling a sense of awkwardness. The majority displayed their curiosity and then got back to whatever it was they were doing. Still, there was one man who smiled and gestured at a vacant part of the floor for me to sit on.

I formed the impression that the cell had been allocated to the highly educated. They were wearing smart attire, just as I was. In the tiny patch of light that came in from a small opening in the roof, I noticed he was wearing a pair of worn-out, black, leather shoes.

When he extended his hand and told me his name, I got the faintest whiff of scent, which was all but overcome by his body odour. Given the number of people crammed into a room of approximately three metres wide by four metres tall, and the lack of air, the smell of body odour was rife. As I hadn't washed for over a week, I was probably as bad as anyone. The feel of his hand confirmed to me that he'd never done any kind of manual work in his life

I was going to tell him my name was Mosa Abu-Rgheff, when I thought better of it and gave him my formal title instead. From the way he smiled and nodded, I could tell I'd impressed him.

"Doctor?" he said, inquisitively, "In what subject?"

I gave him the subject of my PhD. I remarked that I worked at the university, to which he smiled and nodded as if he'd known this all along.

Out of politeness as much as anything, I asked him where he worked. And wouldn't you just know it, he worked at the same place as me. This was either a massive coincidence or they'd deliberately targeted academics.

"Are you a doctor yourself?" I asked, just to keep the conversation alive.

"I'm a professor, actually."

"In what subject?"

"Economics."

This had given me the information I was looking for; he was a fellow academic.

I took a look round at everyone, sat chatting in a civilised manner. While making it clear that I wanted to continue conversing with the professor, I listened in on the conversations going on around me. Politics was a pretty popular subject. And some were vehemently against the new Saddam Hussein regime.

"Why are you here?" I asked, seeking to confirm my theory that everyone in the cell had expressed a political opinion in some shape or form.

He laughed and said I was the kind of man that liked to get straight to the point, which was a pretty accurate conclusion to draw. I smiled politely and, feeling a little awkward, apologised for being so blunt.

He waved away my apologies, lowered his voice and told me he was a member of the communist party.

This made perfect sense. There were many other countries where this would label him a troublemaker, which made me think that my detention was unfair. I put this to the back of my mind and followed up by asking how long he'd been detained. His reply filled me with surprise.

"Oh, many, many years."

I didn't know what to make of this. To me, this meant at least ten or twenty, but the understanding is entirely subjective. However, sensing I was already close to the mark, I decided not to risk asking any further questions.

"Since 1970. It was mid-1970 when they took me."

At first, this surprised me. Just looking at him, I would never have guessed this. His attire didn't look eleven years old, meaning he must have had visitors that brought him new clothes and razor blades.

"Can you tell me what happened, friend?"

I didn't have much of a clue as to what he was referring. "What happened, when?"

"During the 1970s."

"Oh." I took a deep breath. "Where do you want me to start?"

He said to start at the very beginning as we had all the time in the world to talk about it.

So I told him everything I knew, about Iraq, the world in general and my own circumstances. I hesitated before mentioning my capture in 1973, but I knew he'd be interested and if it slipped out later, he'd ask me why I hadn't told him before.

He had no idea about the coup in 1973. He listened so attentively that he reminded me of my daughters listening to Hussein. He had many questions, such as where I was detained, how the guards acted, and even the quality of the food. I told him how bad it was. He laughed and said he thought the food in here might be marginally better.

Everyone turned round to see who was going against the norm. One or two of them smiled and laughed too, although we could clearly see that they were perplexed. I could tell from their faces

165

that they were wondering just what there was to laugh about in such terrible conditions.

I made another joke. I said the amenities there were terrible too. He answered that it might be true, but there was only one toilet in the centre. There was a shower, but no hot water.

There was a break in the conversation. We had shared as much information as we were willing at this stage. For some reason, I hadn't described the way I'd been hung up ad tortured in 1973. Perhaps I had an internal voice that told me to beware. This was a person I'd just met. He gave the impression he was trustworthy, but I couldn't be sure. Perhaps later on, after . . . . A thought struck me.

I looked around at everyone, resting my eyes on each individual for as long as I could without arousing suspicion. The professor noticed and made some kind of joke, that wasn't all that funny. Then I asked him: "You said you'd been here since 1970?"

The professor nodded. "Yes, that is correct."

"What about everyone else in here? Have they been here for as long?"

He nodded to himself in the way people do when they've worked out your train of thought. I could tell he was reluctant to say it. "Yes. I'm afraid so, my friend. There have been one or two new arrivals and a the odd departure, but on the whole—I'm sorry to say this my friend but, you'd better get yourself used to the idea that you're going to be here for quite some time."

The room fell silent. Like a pack of vultures, everyone turned to see how I would react. I just smiled and shrugged it off like it was nothing, but this was only a front to hide what I was really thinking.

In a rare moment of quiet, I thought about the implications of this revelations and how I would cope if I was away for as long as the professor had been. A man reached across and patted my shoulder to gain my attention.

He initiated a conversation by asking me where I'd got my PhD, to which I replied by telling him I'd studied at one of the UK's top universities.

He appeared to be impressed with this and nodded in acknowledgement. There followed a short break in the conversation, before he introduced himself by saying he was a captain, working for the national airline.

There was another break in the conversation, long enough for me to conclude that it was over and consider how I was going to get things back on track. Then, completely out of the blue, he started talking about literature and told me the last novel he had read was *Wuthering Heights* by Emily Bronte. He said it was a good book and recommended I give it a try. He regretted having to leave it half read and was determined to finish it when he got out, even if that meant starting again from page one.

He talked for quite some time, during which I wasn't always paying to close attention to what he was saying. Instead, my thoughts kept drifting back to my family, when we'd all sit at midday every Friday to watch shows that we all liked such as *Little House on the Prairie*, *Love Boat* and *Avengers*. The original English version was kept intact, but there were Arabic subtitles.

I then got to thinking about my wife, who was working at 'Baghdad International School'. Her school was under the umbrella of ESCWA, which stands for Economic, Scientific and Cultural Organization of Western Asia. I did make an effort listen to my new friend, but couldn't stop myself from continuing with this train of thought.

Sometimes, she used to arrive home late because she'd been to the ESCWA library to take out some video tapes for us all to watch. We had this old video recorder to play them on. We spent many happy hours watching these videos together, laughing and joking, snacking on food that my wife had so lovingly prepared. We especially enjoyed this in the winter months when it was dark outside. Then the thought occurred to me that by the time I got out, my daughters might think themselves too old for these nights, preferring to go out with their friends instead. I shifted my attention back to my friend, before he noticed that I was getting choked up.

Chapter 10

A few days after my transfer, a guard entered the cell and told me to follow him. He banged on the door of the office that I'd been in when I'd first arrived and nudged me inside. At the back of the room, there was a metal shelving unit. There were bundles of clothes on each shelf and there, in the middle was one for me. "Your brother sent them in for you," the guard said, holding the door open for me to exit.

Although I wasn't all that keen on changing in front of twenty strangers, I did feel much better afterwards. It was comforting to think that back home, my family were thinking of me and had gone out of their way to make things a tiny bit better.

After changing, I sat on the floor and again thought about how lucky I was to have a family such as mine. It had slipped my mind that I hadn't changed since the morning I last saw my wife, but not theirs. Then a thought struck me; why had my brother sent the clothes in and not my parents? This was most unusual.

I went over and over, trying to think of reasons, but nothing seemed feasible. With nothing to do all day, it's hard not to fall into this trap. I had left them in poor condition, but I couldn't find anything to be unduly concerned about. I sat for a while mulling things over, thinking about how they'd looked or what they'd said on a particular day. As I could find no evidence at all, I assumed it must have been for some other reason and moved on to something else.

This sent my thoughts along a particular path, and I spent the rest of the day thinking about my childhood, my education and the time

I'd spent in the UK. I enjoyed all of these, and they were great memories, but nothing compared to the day my daughters were born; not even my marriage.

I struck up a conversation with the professor and we spent an hour or so talking, mostly about politics, until lights out at 10 pm.

From then on, I conversed with the professor regularly. We tried to keep our voices down whenever we risked falling deeper into trouble than we already were. The guards came and went all the time, and we both assumed that we'd gone unnoticed, until a one burst in and told me to get to my feet.

"We're moving you," the guard said, tugging on my sleeve. The doors clanged shut behind me, and he told me to turn and face the way I'd come in. Outside the last door on the right, he told me to halt.

If the last cell was bad, this was on a whole new level. The air stank of faeces. Just like before, there were twenty or so people crammed into a cell that was roughly 3 metres by 4 metres.

And, as there was no fresh air, there was a high level of humidity.

The guard pushed me inside and the door clanged shut. As his footsteps receded, I took the first look at my new cellmates. Everyone looked like they had given up and were void of hope. There were puddles of urine scattered around the floor, which some people had little choice but to sit in.

I tried to make eye contact with whoever seemed the least bit amiable, but I received nothing in return. Stepping through the squalor, I recalled the things I'd heard about Japanese concentration camps of WW2.

I found a piece of floor beside one of the urine stains and made my way across the room. No one looked up or even acknowledged my presence. I sat down and took a good look round. As hopeless and destitute as they all were, I got a feeling that they were well-educated people just as before. There were, however, a group of men sat in the corner, distancing themselves from the others. I knew right from the start that I had to be wary of these.

I made an attempt at conversing with the man sat beside me. To be fair, he did make a short-lived attempt to be sociable, but it was obvious that he was too weak to think about the issues of the day.

Following this, I sat for hours, contemplating, wondering if I would soon abandon hope like the rest of them. I was determined not to let this happen. Whenever I felt despair creeping in, I thought of my family back home. I missed everyone, but my wife, daughters and Hussein the most. Thinking of them gave me all the strength I needed to get through this, however long that might be.

It soon got dark and the cell vibrated with the sound of snoring. I tried to relax and even managed an hour or so, until I was awoken by the most vile smell.

It smelt like all the sewers in Baghdad had been emptied in the middle of the cell. I looked around at everyone, seeking some answers. One or two of them were awake, but they appeared to be oblivious to the smell. The smell lingered on for hours, but it didn't prevent me from drifting back to sleep.

I woke up to find the snoring had ceased and the people in my vicinity were awake, staring silently at the ceiling. The smell had come back with a vengeance, but once again, no one appeared to notice. I glanced at the man nearest to me, but as I did so, I noticed a different man, squatting in the corner. Everyone had moved as far away from him as they could.

A minute or two later, he stood up, looked around apologetically and sealed the plastic bag he was holding. Without saying a word to anyone, he took the bag and left the cell, walking, as far as I could gather, in the direction of the toilet.

Even with everything I'd been through previously, I found the conditions unbearable. Along with the stench of faeces, there was also body odour to contend with. I knew I was as bad as anyone.

I noticed someone leave the cell. He returned ten minutes later, dripping wet, but invigorated. I enquired as to the shower's whereabouts and if he felt better for it. He said that the water was freezing, because it was December and the temperature sometimes dropped to -5 C at night, but once he'd got over the shock, it was well worth it.

I had no hesitation in following his lead. The shower was more popular than I'd imagined, and I had to join a queue, with five people in front of me. As my fellow prisoner had told me, I felt much better afterwards. At least for an hour or so, anyway. So, I decided to shower twice a week. It's surprising how refreshed this made me feel, both inside and out.

It was while I was queuing for the shower, that I came across a man who acted friendly towards me. As we had the same routine, we saw each other every day, so got to know each other quite well. Then we got talking about our personal lives, where we'd come from, what we did for a living and other things like that.

He told me he was a physician in the army. I showed an interest, and he then went on to give me the name of the residential area in which he lived. I was surprised to find that it was the same area I lived in. This created a bond between us, which, in that setting, was important to both of us. However, when I was back in the cell, thinking about things in the dark, I realised that they might be targeting our area and there were probably others too. It seemed that no one was safe.

My acquaintance with the physician soon became invaluable. Owing to the unsanitary conditions and lack of nutritious food, I fell ill. There wasn't any need for concern to begin with. My temperature rose, and a minute after I returned from the shower, I was saturated in sweat. Then gradually, my condition deteriorated until it became apparent to everyone that I needed help.

One of the guards alerted the physician to my state. He came right away and stayed with me for the rest of the day. By nightfall, I'd also developed problems with my teeth and gums. He said he didn't like the look of this, so refused to leave me alone to deteriorate further. He stayed with me all day and all night for a few days. I won't ever forget the way he sat there, offering me comfort and encouraging my recovery when I felt as sick as I ever had. His distant voice kept creeping into my head, preventing me from slipping away into oblivion.

Thanks to the care and goodwill of the physician, my condition soon improved. I decided I should attempt to get to know a few people, despite my natural instinct to keep away from anyone in such poor health. As I suspected, they were all academics.

I noticed a man to my left who had isolated himself from the rest of the group. He looked like he could do with some cheering up, so I searched for a possible route between all the people sat on the floor and made my way across the room.

As I suspected, he turned out to be a friendly, sociable type of man. We had much in common. He told me that he had a PHd in physics, which he'd attained from a university in Germany. After exchanging stories about our academic lives, the topic turned to our loved ones at home. A veil of sadness descended on each of us as we thought about what we'd been deprived of.

He was the first to snap out of the trance. He told me how much he missed his wife and children. He said he feared for their safety, even though they were as far away as Germany.

As I had already come to the conclusion that no one was safe from the regime, I could empathise with him. I offered him as much succour as I could and the encountered ended with us both deep in thought.

They all had the same pasty, hopeless expression, meaning I hadn't previously been able to gauge their age. Therefore, I was surprised to find that they were all older, some I might even describe as elderly.

They were indeed all educated, but that doesn't mean they'd kept their sense of decorum. In the squalor, some had lowered their standards, used foul language and often spoke of violence. Some of them were drug addicts, so had the tendency to abandon their sense of reason for something wholly malevolent and unpredictable. Therefore, when a guard opened the door and shoved a boy of approximately 13 years inside, I feared for him.

As soon as the doors shut, he slumped onto the floor, dropped his elbows onto his knees and stared through everyone at the wall ahead. Completely out of the blue, one of the men that I now knew to be drug addicts, got to his feet and approached the boy. He dropped his hand on the boy's shoulder, whispered something in his ear and retreated, laughing. Someone had to keep an eye on the boy, and that person should be me.

I gave him a friendly smile and he came to sit near me. Following my words of comfort, he appeared to perk up for the rest of the day. All the time though, I could see the older men, and in particular, the drug addicts, leering at him, waiting for their opportunity to pounce and make his life even more miserable than it already was.

Later on, when the lights were out and everyone had found a patch of floor to lie on, I sat in silent contemplation until my eye lids began to sag, as I often did. While I was deep in thought, I heard an unfamiliar sound. At first, I thought it might be some kind of nocturnal animal, prowling around outside, but the more I listened, the more apparent it became that the noise was originating from inside the cell.

181

In the darkness, I looked around as best I could. Everyone looked to be lying on the floor with their knees tucked up towards their chins. Some asleep, some muttering to themselves, entering some nightly ritual that helped them fight off their insomnia.

The noise came again, louder this time. I heled my breath, cursed the snorers in the cell and tried to ascertain what the noise was and who it was coming from. The sound came again, louder and then again, louder still. Someone was sobbing and doing their utmost to hide it. I knew exactly who it was. I heard him mutter the word 'mother' under his breath. I was about to offer comfort, when he said it again, louder this time. And then—he screamed loud enough for everyone to wake up.

For the rest of the night, they lay in the dark, grumbling to each other and shouting threats at the boy. There only seemed to be me that could hear the sobbing and murmuring that he wanted his mother.

Things didn't improve much once morning came around. He covered his nose as the stench of faeces spread around the cell. He said to someone that the needed he toilet. They threw him one of the plastic bags and pointed to a corner. The boy didn't know what to do with it. Once it became clear, he dropped the bag on the tiny patch of floor in front of him.

When food came, he took his fork and played with it for a while, before reluctantly putting it in his mouth. He'd only taken a couple of mouthfuls when he pushed the plate away and took the tiniest sip of his water. He then raised his chin, screwed his eyes and took a sharp intake of breath, as people do when they experience a sharp pain.

I decided I had to fight my way across to talk to him. As I approached, he shot his hand over his bladder and winced.

Then I understood what was wrong. He'd been so disturbed by the sight of the plastic waste bags, that he'd decided he wasn't going to use them. He was suffering from severe discomfort. I asked one of the others to move up so I could sit next to the boy, which he did at the second time of asking. I put my arm around the boy and told him what amounted to a pack of lies. I said that it would get better and once he'd used the bags a few times, he'd be wondering what he was worried about.

He thanked me for my kind words and told me he was afraid to sleep. I answered with another lie. I said that nights would get better too, and if anyone caused him suffering, a guard would be along straight away. He appeared to take comfort from this, so I continued, trying to make him feel better, although I knew that honesty was the better approach in the long run. I said he'd be out in no time and his mum would make a huge fuss and spoil him for days.

He smiled at this and asked me if I thought that was right. He perked up considerably for the rest of the day, until bedtime came around and someone passed him a plastic bag. This time, I told him that he'd sleep better and holding it in is potentially dangerous. So while he was using the bag, I took centre stage and told everyone a joke that my older brother had told me years before. The boy appeared a minute later, smiling with relief.

184

He lay down close, but not next to me, almost smiling. He'd just about shut his eyes when one of the drug addicts kicked him in the back and told him he was occupying his space. I told the addict to leave him alone. He stared, and for a minute I thought he was going to attack me, until a few of the others told him to let it drop.

As soon as things settled down, the boy started to sob again. I could hear him quite clearly, murmuring to himself, "Mum, I miss you. What have I done?"

So I navigated my way around the sleeping bodies and sat down next to him. I again put my arm around him. This time I said I'd look out for him and he ever felt in need of a friend to just look for me and I'd be there. I reiterated that he'd soon be back with his mum and not to worry. I asked if she was a good cook. He said she was and told me about all his favourite dishes. I said whenever he felt he couldn't cope to think of this and to imagine the meal his mum was going to cook when he got out.

He went quiet for a minute, but I still felt reluctant to leave his side. In a whisper, I asked him what crime he had committed.

He told me that one day, he'd got on his bicycle. He turned onto the road, the same as he did every day to go and sell Samoon (local bread) to the villagers. Everyone loved his mum's bread, and they made a good profit from it. Good enough for his mum to feed a family of four.

Then a car cut in front of him and they took him. I asked him if he could think of any possible reason why they might do this. He said he'd been trying to think of a reason all the time since he was taken, but nothing came to mind.

I told him not to worry and to think of his mum's cooking, as I'd said before. He smiled and rested his head on the cold, hard floor. I retreated back to my space, feeling terrible for lying to him.

It was no more than a few days later when a guard came in and took the boy. I shouted out to the guard to be kind to him. The guard turned round, sniggered and said he couldn't promise anything. Someone asked why not. The guard gave it some thought and then decided to tell us the boy's story.

His family had lived in Koffa, which is a small town to the south of Baghdad. He went on to say that they'd discovered some leaflets calling for a popular uprising against the SH regime inside the Samoon.

The boy called out that this was the doing of the opposition, to which he and his mother had no connection. The guard didn't believe him

Chapter 11

One day, a few weeks after I'd been moved, something unusual occurred. The guards regularly patrolled up and down the corridor, but this time there was a greater sense of purpose. Mixed up with the sound of the guard's heavy boots, there was a softer sound, which could only mean one thing.

A rare moment of silence descended as we listened in, trying to judge if they were heading our way. When they stopped outside the door, those of use with a sharp sense of hearing knew precisely what to expect. I couldn't believe that in the comparatively short time I'd been there, that I was as excited as everyone else about the arrival of a new inmate.

The door swung open and the guard pushed him inside. The guard mumbled something and then stood by as our new cellmate stumbled the cell.

I felt sorry for him, because this wasn't the greatest of starts. Just about managing to stay on his feet, the man looked up and gave everyone the kind of awkward smile that people often produce to hide their embarrassment.

In the cramped conditions, I tried to move up to make room for him, which led to an angry response from the man next to me. He didn't like what little space he had being encroached on further still. With my shoulder pressed firmly into my neighbour's, I gestured at the newcomer to come and sit beside me.

It reminded me of my first day. To my surprise, the demeanour of the man beside me, and indeed everyone else in the cell, changed the minute they saw his face close-up. Some smiled at him and others reacted angrily, shaking their heads and saying he wasn't welcome. He followed a pathway from the door to the wall and sat down beside me, in the space we'd just created.

For a while, I became the meat in a sandwich. The man that had been present all along reached across my shoulders and patted the newcomer on the back. He then asked him what he'd done this time. On hearing his story, a few of the others turned around and shook their heads in disbelief. I could only conclude that he'd been there before.

I said hello and offered him my hand. As we made eye contact, I got a good look at him for the first time. I estimated him to be in his late twenties, which in this company, made him very young indeed. He had shoulder-length hair, which was greasy and unkempt.

I tried to initiate a conversation, but he just looked at me without making any kind of response. I spoke again, louder this time. The man on my left tapped me on the shoulder and offered up an explanation for his silence.

As it turned out, the newcomer was a student in the university's medical faculty. He often appeared and then went again after no more than a month or so.

They had tortured him on more than one occasion, which had caused him severe trauma. He'd lost his mind and was now totally mute. He didn't even know his own name.

The man told me that on one occasion, they released him near to his house. However, he was in no fit state to find his home, so he just wandered round, seemingly at random. A few days later, they went to check on him and found him sleeping rough. They returned him to the cell until the next time he was released, and the same thing happened again. It was my opinion that he should have been in hospital rather than a detention centre, where no one made any concessions.

In this cell, as with every cell I'd been locked up in, time crept by. During the night, everything was exaggerated. I spent the time fretting about my family, wondering if I was going to be held for years like the professor in the previous cell. If I was detained for anywhere near as long as he'd been, my daughters would be all but grown-up when I next saw them.

Some time after I was first detained, maybe a few weeks, but I wasn't sure exactly, there was a kerfuffle outside. Everyone paid attention, trying to ascertain what was going on. I would later go on to find out that this occurred at roughly 11 pm.

Some of my cellmates walked to the far wall. They thought that if they pressed their ear against the wall, they'd get a better idea of what was going on. There was little need for this, though.

The chatter of excited guards in the yard was soon drowned out by the noise of an oncoming vehicle, a large one by the sound of it. The vehicle came to a halt, with the engine left running. Then there was another voice, and the engine revved up again. It grew louder for thirty seconds or so until it stopped altogether, probably outside the entrance. The doors clanged open and what sounded like forty or so people climbed out. We were all nonplussed as to who they might be and what they were doing there.

It felt like I'd only been asleep for a matter of minutes, although for all knew, it could have been hours, when I awoke again. I sat up to look around and to my astonishment found the cell absolutely teeming with people. I asked the man beside me, who was sat with this back to the wall, shaking his head, and he told me that they were the people we'd heard earlier. "Who are they?" I whispered.

The man beside me continued to shake his head. "Don't have a clue, but it really wouldn't surprise me if they were prisoners of war."

This theory seemed plausible enough, so I accepted it as the truth and, with my curiosity appeased, soon went back to sleep.

I woke up again, to find the newcomers gone. A few of my cellmates had seen them being herded out, but they didn't know where. I decided it was time that I took a shower.

I'd only just stepped into the corridor when I saw them all packed into the cell opposite.

"What is it?" someone whispered over my shoulder.

Putting my shower on hold, I stepped back into the cell, leaving the door open for everyone to see.

Some people behind me had started whispering, exchanging theories. Then everyone went quiet as we watched a young chap in the cell opposite take a pen from his pocket and begin to write. We all observed the pen move across and then down the page, without uttering a word. He looked up at us and raised the paper for us to see.

We were actually arrested in Basra and brought here

There was a scrawling noise behind me, as if someone was writing on a piece of paper. I looked over my shoulder, to find he was holding up a reply. *But Why?*

And so the conversation continued. It turned out that most of the elderly people in the group were hostages. They were being used as bargaining chips and would only be released if they surrendered their sons/relatives to the Saddam Hussein regime.

If they were anything like me, they would never even contemplate surrendering their children. They were going to be hostages until either the regime realised it was a waste of time and resources or they got old and died.

I thought back to the time I'd just returned home from the UK after completing my PhD. My mother took me to visit her older sister plus another relative in Basra. It was a journey that's been etched in my mind forever as that's when I first broached the news that I was going to be married.

I hadn't seen or heard from that relative for a long time, and for all I knew he could have been arrested along with the rest of them.

I asked the man behind me if I could borrow his pen and a piece of paper. I scrawled down my relative's name and held it up to for the people in the cell opposite to read. I wanted to know if he was safe.

An elderly man smiled and waved. A combination of elation and relief prompted me to continue the silent conversation. I wrote again, several times, asking if someone I knew was alive or not. Each time the man smiled and replied in the affirmative.

He looked like an amicable man, whom I could trust. So I continued, this time asking him to act as a messenger. I told him that if he'd heard previously that I'd been killed, to pass on a message asking the recipient to tell my wife to stop waiting for my return. It was the most gut-wrenching thing I've ever had to do.

His eyes filled with despair; tears dripped onto his long grey beard. He raised both his hands to the ceiling and mumbled a few words that I couldn't quite catch.

"Excuse me, sir." An elderly man, who looked vaguely familiar raised his hand to catch my attention.

I smiled at him and asked what I could do.

He walked up to the door, dodging round all the watching bodies until he was just centimetres away from me.

He asked me to show him the name I'd written, once more. I handed it to him through the bars and watched him examine each word in turn. He passed it back and nodded. "Sir, I think I know your wife."

I couldn't see any positives to take from this revelation. "How?"

"I'm a neighbour of yours. I live in a nearby street."

This explained why he looked familiar. I'd most likely encountered him at the shops or walking along the pavement some time. I couldn't understand why he was captured if the arrests were made in Basra. He replied that he'd been away on business and had been taken as a result of an unfortunate coincidence.

"Sir, I have some news."

I felt my entire body tremble

"No sir, it's not bad news. But it isn't good news, either. It's just news."

"Oh." I took a few deep breaths and gave some private thanks to God. "What is it?"

He looked over his shoulder at his cellmates, who were all eavesdropping. "No, not here, he whispered, "can you meet me outside the shower, tomorrow morning at—is 10 am OK?"

"It should be." The truth is that I didn't know if I could make it at that time. To keep the queues to a minimum, we'd allocated each other ten minutes timeslots for the shower. As my regular slot was before 10 am, I'd have to pull a few strings. But hopefully, I'd be able to manage it.

"*It should be*? Can you meet me there or not?"

"Yes. Yes, I will meet you at 10 am."

The man retreated to the back of the cell. I made the short journey back to my own cell, wondering what he might have to say.

The man that went after me to the shower was not particularly nice. Whilst I wouldn't say I'd had any run-ins with him, I knew he'd be stubborn. Still, I had to persuade him by hook or by crook.

I saw him sat on the floor, facing the wall. Lots of inmates did this. I assumed it was to try and find ripples or imperfections in the plaster, which I knew, with a little imagination, could help pass the time. I tapped him on the shoulder and he swung round, scowling.

"Good morning, friend," I said, hoping for the best.

The man shrugged and asked me in a gruff voice, what I wanted.

I did my best to explain to him my predicament, without divulging any of the details. I just said there was someone I knew in a different cell who he had some information for me. To my complete surprise, he didn't dismiss it out of hand; he made a pause before he said no. However, this told me he was in two minds and with a little persuasion, he could be open to the idea.

Recalling that this man had expressed some views that could be perceived as inflammatory, I played on this and said I wouldn't forget it when we got out. I told him there were only a few of us that dared to stand up to the regime, and we had to help each other out.

"Well, OK," he said, nodding his head, "but just this once. And you owe me one."

I smiled, thanked him and said I would be forever in his debt.

So the next morning, I waited for him to return from the shower before heading for the door. I nodded and thanked him once again as we passed, to which he replied that it was no problem at all. I was starting to get the feeling that this confrontation might lead to some kind of alliance.

Only three people stood waiting outside the shower. I always felt disappointed when the queue was short, but this time it made me worried too. What if the man failed to show up on time? He might think I didn't care and not make an effort again.

I waited patiently, continually looking over my shoulder and listening out for the sound of approaching footsteps. When the man ahead of me in the queue entered the shower, and there was still no sign, I started to panic. But I soon decided that there was no reason to be concerned providing I had a contingency plan, so I got to work right away.

I was still deep in thought when I felt a tap on my shoulder. He took me a few paces along a corridor that I'd never been down before, and into a storeroom that was full of tinned food. It was lucky that we ate in the evening and not at lunch or breakfast.

He carefully closed the door and walked towards me through the darkness, choosing not to switch the light on.

When he was near enough for me to feel his breath on my face, he lowered his voice to a whisper and said, "As I said, I have some information about your wife."

I opened my mouth, but no words would come. I was both astounded and out of my mind with worry. My wife had made great progress in adjusting to life in Iraq as much as she had, but she was still a British woman living in a foreign country.

Being as amiable as she is, my wife had many friends in the neighbourhood and had been admired by everyone. Then word got around that I had been detained and all that changed overnight. Her so called friends now looked at her with disdain and crossed the road to avoid her. This, I assumed, was for fear of reprisals from the dictator.

Our neighbour glanced over his shoulder, to check for eavesdroppers. "I saw your wife," he whispered, "she was taking your daughters to school about two months before my trip to Basra. My friend, your wife is still living in your house."

As soon as I heard this, my eyes started to well. I wanted to throttle her for putting herself in so much danger. Her safety was my biggest concern. But at the same time, I felt honoured to have such a courageous wife. "But what about my daughters? Are they OK?"

"Well, they were when I last saw her. As far as I know, they are safe and sound at school. My friend, you are married to a woman with the heart of a lion. You should be very proud."

"I know, " I said, my voice full of emotion, "and I am."

"Well, that's all I have to say. It goes without saying that you won't breathe a word to anyone."

"Of course, it goes without saying."

He turned to reach for the door handle. "Better be getting back."

I had so many emotions running around my head that I really didn't know what to feel. Should I feel proud for showing so much courage, or angry for putting herself at risk? In the end, I decided to be proud, but I'd make the point later that she shouldn't put herself such danger on my account again.

Chapter 12

At the start, it was just the conditions that bothered me, but as time passed, I became tired of seeing the same people day in day out. I'd got to know everything there was to know about them, just through observing how they lived. What time they awoke, what type of food they liked and what they pushed back across the floor for the guards to take away. I'd even started to notice their nightly toileting routines.

I spoke to everyone as often as I could, but it was just to pass the time. I wasn't particularly fond of any of them. I got tired of listening to the same regurgitated stories. But then, with nothing at all happening, fresh anecdotes were scarce. I was probably as just guilty as anyone, in fact, I knew I was. I must have told every one of them about my past at some time or other. Sometimes an idea would come to mind, and I'd seek out the person that would be most interested to hear it. But the enthusiasm only lasted a matter of minutes before there was a deathly silence and we'd either end the conversation or go over old, well-trodden ground.

I was sat in the squalor, watching the flies buzz around, head drooped, when I heard voices in the corridor, two of them by the sound of it. The sound of jangling keys sent everyone into a frenzy.

The guard nodded in my direction and made everyone clear a path so he could get to me. He seized the back of my collar and told me to get up. "Your day has come," he said and led me along the path he'd just created.

With one foot through the door, I looked over my shoulder and said goodbye. This wasn't the first time I'd been told it was my day. In fact, everyone had been called at some time or another, only to be told there'd been a mistake.

However, this time it just felt different. I'd been there for approaching a year so had gathered my things together a few weeks beforehand. I wanted to be ready if the call came. Of course, it might be another 'mistake', but everything pointed towards it being the real deal this time. Or so I chose to believe.

Once the door had clanged shut, I asked the guard to give me a minute. He sighed, glanced at his watch and replied, "OK, you have one minute."

I turned to wave goodbye to the prisoners from Basra, who had congregated around the door to try and satisfy their curiosity. I turned to go on my way, but I'd only taken one step when I heard the distinct sound of someone crying. I stopped in my tracks to look over my shoulder. The guard sighed and mumbled something inaudible, but didn't force me to go along with him. It seemed I'd struck lucky with the guard today.

I peered in through the bars. The sobbing was coming from an elderly man, and as I focused in, it became clear it was the man with whom I'd left a message. The guard tugged on my sleeve to tell me he had run out of patience.

So, with one last look over my shoulder, hoping for eye-contact, I followed the guard along the corridor towards the entrance.

I felt a tap on my shoulder. I turned round, hoping the guard, who was walking beside me, wouldn't notice. It was a young man, who muttered, "Stand up to them."

I nodded and turned to face the outside world that I could see approaching through the window in front.

As soon as the doors opened, I raised my hand to shield my eyes from the bright sun. The air was warm and dirty. It came as quite an unpleasant shock. I'd become accustomed to the foul-smelling air in the cell and had forgotten the feeling of being outside.

Through the rows of parked cars, I spied a military vehicle. By now, I knew the drill. The guard waiting by the open door was going to push me inside. Sure enough, that's what happened and surprise, surprise, I found myself the meat in a sandwich that reeked to high heaven of sweat and body odour. As the engine started to roll, I asked myself if possibly I had been showering more frequently than they had.

At this stage, I wasn't sure, but there'd been nothing to suggest that I'd soon be making the return journey back to my cell.

I didn't know if they were going to lock me up somewhere overnight or if they were going to take me straight to court. I was surprised when the car pulled up just a short distance from the court. As I stepped out, it made sense. Why would they give me time to think things through and prepare my defence? In this version of a court of law, defence lawyers were not permitted for detainees.

The court was an intimidating place. I had heard that they sat on Wednesdays, with death sentencing being undertook on Fridays.

It wasn't really a trial, more of a formality in which I was sentenced to two years, including the detention period. As I'd been detained for a year already, I had a further year to serve as a prisoner.

So they put me back in the car and took me to prison. Abu-Ghraib was notorious for torture, physical abuse, and worse. I knew it would be tough, but felt confident I'd make it through and emerge stronger for the experience.

An awaiting guard opened the gates for us to enter. I attempted to get a look at my new prison through the windscreen, but I couldn't see anything until the car stopped and I got out. Almost immediately a soldier, carrying a gun, grabbed hold of me and my escorts left the scene.

From the outside, it didn't look like a prison, more like a military fortress. The towering stone walls were interspersed with stone rods, producing a corrugated effect. It told all who saw it that any attempt to escape would be futile and they'd most likely be recovered in a plastic bag.

My first impressions of the interior were that it looked like any other prison. There were long, unwelcoming corridors with tiled floors and cells with cream coloured bars on either side. Most of the doors were open, allowing the guards to see inside so they could take swift action if needs be. Unlike the guards in the detention centre, these carried rifles. They wore military uniforms, helmets and all, like they were about to go into battle. It was clear that they wouldn't hesitate to pull the trigger, should any prisoner give them the tiniest excuse.

Our echoing footsteps clapped against the floor until we stopped. They pushed me inside a cell that was bare apart from a bed that ran along the side wall. Then they walked off, laughing and joking as the clang from the door reverberated along the corridor.

I use the word cell, but it was really a cage. There were bars, made of wrought iron, on all four walls. In the distance, I could hear screaming, which probably came from torture rooms.

I sat on my bed and dropped my face into my hands; I'd sunk to an all-time low.

Unlike in the detention centre, there were no others to talk to and to observe night and day. Everywhere smelt of professionalism and a lethal intolerance. I could see how it could quickly become too much for some people. Once over, this might have been me, but my previous experiences had made me strong. I knew that if I kept my head down and stayed out of trouble that in a years' time, I would be reunited with my family, and the ordeal would be over.

Things didn't get any better at night. I was made to sleep with my head to the door, so that passing guards could look in to check I was asleep.

In the distance, the wailing and screaming went on. I'd now heard enough to conclude without a shadow of a doubt, that somewhere, someone was being tortured. However bad things were for me and everyone around me, they were not as bad as they were for the person sat, standing or hung up in that room.

I spent the remainder of that night laid awake on the bed, on a mattress that could just as easily pass for a soiled blanket. I thought about everything that had happened. With those experiences behind me, I felt a certain amount of apathy. Like a hardened criminal, I was used to being locked up and had all the necessary skills to survive.

I did drift off, but I'd made the subconscious decision not to sleep soundly, because if I did, I would pay for it when I was sat with my back against the wall during the day. When you're locked up, backache is the last thing you need.

When everyone was officially awake, a man in the adjacent cell tapped on the bars and whispered to me. I crept forwards to find his arm outstretched to shake my hand. I was just about to make an attempt to accept his offer of friendship when a guard appeared from nowhere. In no time at all, my neighbour was being dragged towards a room at the end of the corridor. To his credit, he made no protestations of any kind.

Minutes later, the corridor filled with more screaming, if anything even more disconcerting than the previous day. I couldn't help closing my eyes to try and picture the scene, and to prepare myself for his return.

The screaming went on for most of the day. No sooner had it stopped then I could hear him wincing as he made the long walk back to his cell.

I wanted to try to reach out, to shake his hand and apologise, but I knew that in doing so I'd put us both in the torture room. So reluctantly, I dropped onto my bed and came to terms with my guilty conscience.

Several days later, a guard burst in and ordered me to follow. As we passed the last cell, he told me without turning his head, that I had a visitor.

This could be anyone. It might even be some kind of senior official coming to tell me that my plight was about to become even worse. But with each footstep, I managed to convince myself more and more that it was my wife. I imagined she'd be waiting with my daughters, however improbable It might be.

I continued towards the visiting area, hoping it would be my wife or perhaps my parents or Hussein. The last thing I wanted to see was—.

"Mosa!"

My mum emerged through the doorway, closely followed by my dad's cousin, whom I knew well. She opened her arms wide and tried to rush towards me, but as she did so, stumbled. She held onto the back of someone's chair until my dad's cousin lunged forwards to stop her falling. The chair's occupant turned round and told her to be careful.

My mum apologised to him and continued on her way, taking it steady this time. She rested her fingers on the back of each chair, whilst trying to avoid prodding its occupant.

I tried to remain calm as I walked past all the watching eyes to a table in the far corner. Once I was there, I couldn't contain myself any longer.

"It's so good to see you," I said, wiping my eyes with the back of my hand.

My mum stood up, opened her arms as wide as they would go and hugged me for all she was worth.

Words can't express how overjoyed I felt.

"Mum, it's so good to see you," I said, trying to hide my emotions for fear of looking weak in front of the other prisoners.

My dad's cousin sidled up behind her, asked if she was OK, and took a chair from a nearby vacant table.

He shook my hand, said it was good to see me and engaged with me in a short conversation. I described the conditions, and he told me about this business. It was a very man-to-man chat, which my mother didn't want to participate in.

Although I really wanted to talk to my mother, I enjoyed hearing about his business. It was good to hear about something external, that wasn't related to prison. I could see he enjoyed it too, but once we'd stopped talking, an expression of despair descended on him.

My mum put her arm around him, as if she was trying to console him about something. "Where's Dad?" I said, attempting to dispel a tinge of worry that had just appeared in the back of my mind.

Although I was addressing my dad's cousin, my mum replied for him, saying my dad didn't feel up to it.

For the first time, I noticed a slur in her words.

I looked inquisitively at my dad's cousin and noticed tears rolling down his face. He wiped his cheek with his finger and tried to pretend it hadn't happened.

As soon as the opportunity arose, I lowered my voice to a murmur and asked my mum why he was crying. She just said he'd been under a lot of stress at work, adding that there was nothing for me to worry about.

It felt like they'd only just arrived when a whistle blew to tell the visitors to leave and the prisoners to go back to their cells.

My mum stumbled again as she got up, so she called out to a guard and asked him if there was a short cut. When the guard came closer, she repeated herself and explained that she'd hurt her leg.

The guard just shrugged and shook his head. As he turned to walk back to his station, my mum stopped him. "I have something for you," she said, delving deep into her pocket.

The guard looked at her without making a comment.

"Here." She produced some gold holy Quran that she'd bought from Hajj. The guard thought for a moment, then took the gold and guided them through.

As soon as my cell door clanged shut and the guard walked away, I dropped onto my bed and mulled over what had just happened.

I was happy to see my mum, and my dad's cousin's presence was a pleasant surprise. At first, my dad's absence didn't worry me all that much, I was more curious than anything. But if there was nothing to worry about, then why had he cried like that?

A week later, I had another visit. This time, it was my wife who sat at a table waiting for me. As soon as she saw me, she stood up and waved.

She was with my cousin, who often accompanied her as most of my siblings worked during the day.

I kissed my wife and said hello to my cousin. I enjoyed hearing all the news, but I was especially keen to hear about my daughters, who were making rapid progress at school. I scanned the mail that she always brought and tucked some technical journals away to read later. Then I told her that something was worrying me.

She turned glum and asked what was bothering me.

I told her about my mum, how she struggled to walk and slurred her words. My wife paused before saying she'd had a bout of the flu recently, and was probably still suffering from the effects of that.

"My dear, are you sure there's nothing else?"

My wife nodded. "Yes, I'm sure. There's absolutely nothing for you to worry about."

I noted that she used the exact same phrase as my mum had.

I then told her about my dad's cousin crying when I mentioned my dad to him. "He's not ill is he, my dad? My cousin hadn't been told to keep quiet about something, had he?"

My wife shook her head. "Not as far as I know. He hadn't seen you for a long time. You know how much he likes you, he was probably feeling a bit emotional, that's all."

This appeased my concerns to an extent, but I could tell from the look on her face that there was more. I could see I wouldn't get any more information from my wife, so I asked my cousin the same question.

He gave the same answer as my wife. I decided to let it drop and try to stop worrying over what was probably nothing.

When my sister and her husband next came to visit, we sat outside in the garden that the prison manager sometimes let me use. I was delighted to discover that they had brought some homegrown fruit and nuts. I knew I should save them for later, to help pass the time when I was alone in my cell, but they were so delicious that I couldn't help eating some there and then.

All my family came to visit regularly, so I was never alone with my thoughts for that long. However, only one of my colleagues came to visit. I had a theory that this was because they were afraid of reprisals from Saddam.

Following my wife's next visit a few weeks later, I sat outside in the prison officer's garden, reading my post. I was still in high spirits from seeing her, and although the post was just mundane stuff, it maintained my good mood as it reminded me of her.

I had my head buried in a letter, absorbing each and every word, when I heard someone running towards me. I looked over my shoulder to see the prison officer puffing and panting as he approached at speed.

"Mosa," he said, trying to catch his breath. "There are some people to see you. Two important looking gentlemen."

I sighed and got to my feet. I had been through this too often to feel any kind of anxiety.

However, as soon as I set eyes on them, I knew it was not as I'd thought. They said they'd been sent from the president's office and that they'd come to help.

"But I haven't done anything wrong, I shouldn't have been taken to start with. Can you tell me why that is?"

Chapter 13

1983

After a year in prison and another in detention, it seemed almost surreal that in a matter of hours I'd be at home, drinking tea with my family. I thought there might be a period of adjustment, during which time my family might see some changes in me. I hoped this wouldn't be the case and I'd find everyone to be well and in high spirits.

The sentry raised the gates and bade me farewell. This was the first time anyone outside my family had spoken to me with respect for two years. It was with a great sense of pride then that I stood beside the road with dust blowing into my eyes. I stared along the road, looking out for approaching cars.

Back in 1973 when I'd been released, my family were none the wiser. I had to hail a taxi and rush inside to find money to pay him. This time it was different. My family had been notified in advanced, and my brother was coming to collect me. And take me home.

I wasn't sure at first. I raised my hand to shield my eyes from the dust and peered along the road at the car that was growing bigger and bigger by the second. By the time it had turned onto the street that the prison gives out as its official address, I knew it was my brother. We waved, my brother mirroring my own smile.

He got out, ran around the car and opened the passenger door for me. As I was about to step inside, he pulled me back and gave me a brotherly hug. He patted my back and said it was good to see me.

Just as the engine revved up, the prison gate behind us lifted, and a black military car passed. I hoped the prisoner was as fortunate as I was to have such a loving family to be his source of strength.

I didn't look back, not once. My brother tried to initiate a conversation many times. I tried to be communicative, but I wasn't quite ready to be sociable. My brother noticed this and called my mother to tell her not to make too much fuss when we arrived. I thanked him and relaxed into the seat.

Up until that point, I hadn't given much thought to what would be awaiting me at my parents' house, where we were going. I'd been consumed with the magnitude of the situation and trying come to terms with being a free man again. Some people get used to the regimental lifestyle and find it hard to adjust when they get out. I worried this would happen to me, but as we neared our destination, I managed to dismiss the idea. I didn't feel quite ready to celebrate, though. My brother had done me a great service by phoning ahead to tell my mum. All I wanted to do was to sit on the sofa, drinking tea with my wife. Everything else could wait for another day.

Everyone was waiting for me at my parents'. My mum had told the entire family to gather together for a huge party, but, after my brother's message, it was a much more sober affair. Not only did I feel grateful to my brother, but to my mum too, for being so understanding.

My brother stepped aside to let me walk ahead of him along the path. The garden was like a lush green carpet, and the blossoming trees gave off a smell I'd almost forgotten about. There were even one or two birds chirping away.

I creaked open the back door, inched it forwards and poked my head around. Despite my attempt at surprising them all, my eldest sister, who was in the kitchen preparing some snacks, saw me. "Mosa!", she cried, running across to hug me and kiss me on the cheek.

The noise carried into the living room, and everyone came flooding into the kitchen to greet me. By the time I'd said hello to everyone, my ribs hurt from being tightly hugged, and my back felt sore from all the patting it had received. We filed back into the living room to have, at my mother's insistence, a quiet catch up.

The minute I stepped into the living room and saw my dad's armchair occupied by someone else, I knew something was wrong. Then my eyes were drawn to my dad's picture. It was hung on the wall, in the same place, just as I'd seen it in my mind's eye, over and over. Upon careful inspection, I noticed a strange dark line running across the middle. I filled up with foreboding and took a step forward, hoping that I'd made a mistake, or my mum would offer up a simple explanation. But no. As I moved closer, I saw the dark line was, in fact, the horizontal part of a cross, made from a dark cloth.

The room spun around me. All the happy, chattering people became increasingly distant as I sunk beneath the surface of a rapidly turning whirlpool. It was too much for me on this day of all days, I had to close my eyes to shut it out . . .

When I came round, I was on the floor, with my head propped up against the side of a chair. My dad had passed away whilst I was inside; life would never be the same again.

My mum rushed to my aid. She was relieved that I was OK, but completely devastated that I'd had to find out in this way. I sobbed in her arms for a while, until she patted my head and asked if I was hungry.

The mood eventually picked up again and we all sat talking, until one by one everyone went home. Suddenly it was just my immediate family and me. My mother yawned and said it was her bedtime.

I sat with my daughters on my lap, talking about school and anything else that they cared to mention. Then they too started rubbing their eyes, and my wife took them from me. "Just one minute," I said, getting to my feet, "there's something I want to do. It's important to me."

My wife gave me an inquisitive kind of smile. "OK."

So I went into the kitchen and made two cups of tea. Then I played out the image that had kept me going through my darkest days. I sat on the sofa, drinking tea with my gorgeous wife and daughters. I started getting a bit emotional.

I spent a few minutes explaining this to her. This took the conversation in a direction that for the time being, I wanted to steer away from. So, when the road outside had gone quiet, and we could hear everyone else in the house snoring, we drank up and went to bed.

It was broad daylight when I awoke. Some people were talking on the street, which I could hear clearly above the sound of passing cars. My wife was sat up in bed, reading a book, not wishing to leave my side.

When we got up, we found my mother on her own in the living room. "So, what happened—to Dad?"

My mum screwed her eyes to hold in her tears before she spoke. Whilst I was in detention, my dad had been very worried about my safety. She said that rumours were circulating of the most barbaric treatment of prisoners. She'd heard that anyone sentenced to death was put into plastic bags and thrown outside their parents' house.

I could see this was hard for her, so I told her she didn't have to continue. The rest of the story could be saved for another time.

But she shook her head and went on. "He was very ill at the end. He passed away, surrounded by all his children and grandchildren. It was just as he would have wanted, apart from Dad's brother being unable to attend. He wasn't well, either."

It all got too much for her and she left the room, apologising to me as she wiped her eyes with the back of her hand.

My wife took over from there. She said it had been very hard on my mum. This didn't surprise me at all, as my dad had been her rock for over 50 years. They'd brought up 10 children together, during war and peace.

They went to Hajj and fetched holy water from the well of Zamzam, which is located within the Masjid Al-haram, in Mecca. She used the holy water to cleanse my dad's body, which in Islam follows specific conventions.

And on top of all this, my mother had been out of her mind with worry about me. As she saw it, there was the possibility of losing her son as well, which weighed heavy on her right up until they received notice of my impending release.

This was very shocking, but it made sense of a lot of things. However, there was still one thing that remained unexplained. "Have you noticed the way my mother slurs her words?"

My wife nodded. "That's something else. Not long after your dad passed away, she suffered a stroke."

I was engulfed by a numbness like I'd never felt before. My wife took me in her arms and said we'd get through it together.

We stayed with my family for a few days. Despite the shocking news, it was a happy time. Everything seemed to be perfectly normal, including my mother's speech. Then one morning, my wife and I were sat in the living room. I looked up at my dad's photo and felt as if my world come tumbling down again.

My wife grasped my hand and said we should go to his grave to lay some flowers. I agreed that this was a good idea, so we started making the arrangements. More than anything, I wanted to ask for his forgiveness for causing him so much pain. My wife said this wasn't necessary and she was probably right, but it was something I had to get off my chest or else I'd never be at peace.

Standing over his grave, I became very emotional. If my wife hadn't been with me, I don't know what I would have done. We stayed all day. As the night drew in, I, at last, felt at peace with myself, so we got in the car and drove back home.

My mum could see I'd been crying when I got back and made a huge fuss. I wanted to tell her to leave me be, because I didn't want to make her relive the pain, but I knew she wouldn't take any notice.

We stayed with my family for another couple of days, before my wife and I decided to go back to our house. This felt like a massive milestone for me. It was like I had been released for real and was a starting point for the rest of my life.

I'd only just stepped into the house when it all came flooding back. The smell of my wife's cleaning fluid made me feel at home straight away. Then there were the little things such the flowers and ornaments that made a great deal to her. We all sat huddled around for a while, doing more catching up and making plans. Then my daughters went to their bedroom to play with a new game they had; their laughter made me feel like I'd never been away.

We let things calm down for the next few weeks. To begin with, my mother, plus many other relatives and friends, came to visit almost every day. But then my mum decided of her own accord that we needed to be on our own and told everyone else. I was grateful to her for this. Recalling how my brother had read my thoughts on the way home, it made me think, once again, that I was lucky to be part of such a close family where everyone knew each other inside out.

My wife and I were sat outside one sunny afternoon when she put down her drink and turned sombre.

"What is it?" I asked.

"It's something that happened while you were away. Something that I think you should know about."

"Tell me, please do. I want to know everything."

She took a deep breath and started at the beginning. The day after I'd been taken, two state security officers came into the house, searching for something. She said she'd been terrified and held our daughters tightly, but she was polite to them. She could see no reason not to be.

"That's terrible, I had no idea."

"It was quite an ordeal. But there's more."

She took a sip of her drink before replying, saying that they took the box that I kept all my letters in. She was referring to a box I used for letters from my friends in Baildon and my colleagues at the school I worked at before we moved to Baghdad.

"This is terrible, my dear. I'm so sorry for putting you through all of this. But what I don't understand is, why did they take them?"

My wife shrugged. "I was hoping you could tell me."

She continued with her story. She'd continued to work at Baghdad International School and saw to it that no harm could come to our daughters, but this involved spending some time staying with my family.

I told her she was a good mother and I never doubted that she'd look after our daughters. There was a pause in the conversation, during which time we both had some tea. Then she brought up the subject of her meeting with Saddam.

"I decided to meet the dictator to get some answers, face to face."

"That was a courageous thing to do, but did you not consider the possible consequences?" Once again, I didn't know whether to feel proud or angry with her for putting herself in so much danger on my behalf.

She said it was a decision she hadn't made lightly. She'd thought long and hard about it, and what she should say when she got there.

Saddam sometimes meets ordinary people to discuss their problems. My wife saw this as an opportunity to do something instead of sitting at home, waiting for news.

She described to me the journey and what happened when she arrived. She had to sit in a room with a crowd of people and wait for her turn.

"What did you ask him when you got here?"

She said she'd started by telling him about my PHD and that when I arrived home, unlike many others, I was set on building my country. She added that I was a patriot that loved his country very much.

"Saddam listened to what I had to say and then changed the subject."

"Typical. What did he say?"

"Something about a democratic society."

"Really? He had a nerve."

"You're telling me he did. He spent the next ten minutes or so giving me a lecture. He Completely dismissed my questions about you."

She said she'd heard enough at that point, so just thanked him for his time and went on her way.

After hearing all of this, I didn't know what to do next. Eventually, I decided to take a break for a week or two, whilst I gave everything some thought. More than anything, I was worried about the future safety of my wife and children. My wife suggested that she should leave the school by the end of the academic year, for an indefinite period. Reluctantly, I agreed, so this was the course of action we took.

Once everything had returned to normal, my attention turned to my mother. I asked her to relay to me in greater detail what she'd been told by the doctor. I decided there and then that she was going to have a course of physiotherapy, no ifs or buts. It had done so much good for Hussein a few years earlier.

I didn't enjoy taking her. She was always quiet on the way there, as if she was secretly worried about it. When she emerged from the clinic, I could tell she'd suffered, but we both knew it was short term pain for long term gain. And that's how it turned out; little by little, she began to recover, and in no time at all, she was back to her old self. Well, almost. When the physiotherapy ended, we had a celebration, and my mum said it was going to be like a new start. Little did we know that she'd only be with us for another four years.

Chapter 14

April 1983

Following my release from prison, things soon returned to normal. My wife was at work all day, and my daughters at school. Later on, in the evening, we'd all sit down together and have a family meal, just as we had two years previously. It was about a month later that I started to think about my personal long-term future. I had to decide if I wanted to go back to my old job at the university or find something else. A new post without any reminders of that fateful day when the office receptionist told me I had to report to the state security office. I thought long and hard about this until, eventually, I decided to give it a go at the university and see how it panned out. I had been happy there before this happened, after all

It was a Monday morning when I left the house. I thought it would be good to make it the first day of the week, get me back into the swing of things. It was by no means a foregone conclusion, though. For all I knew, they could have found a perfectly adequate replacement or made the role redundant altogether. I'd been away for two years and a lot could've changed. They were not going to reappoint me out of sentiment, and what's more, I wouldn't expect them to.

So, when I got into the car, I was actually a bit nervous. It reminded me of when I'd first been interviewed four years earlier.

I'd had the foresight to phone in beforehand, so the director was expecting me. It wouldn't have looked good if I'd turned up without warning and demanded my old job back.

The minute I opened the doors and absorbed the distinctive smell that all colleges and universities seem to possess, it all came flooding back. The receptionist was surprised and delighted to see me. We spent a few minutes chatting about nothing important, before I turned to ascend the stairs that led to my old department. After the first flight, it became apparent that I wasn't as fit as I had been.

I passed a few people on the stairs, some unfamiliar and some that remembered me well. A couple of them were overjoyed to see me and wished me luck. So, I was feeling positive when I opened the doors that led to my old department. No one so far had said my role had been filled, so I was optimistic that they'd welcome me with open arms.

As soon as I stepped inside, I noticed a change of atmosphere. Just as I'd expected, there were some new faces, who smiled and returned my greetings as we passed. Most of my old colleagues were sat around a table, having a meeting of sorts. When one of them looked up, I smiled and waved, but he didn't acknowledge me. I assumed that he just hadn't seen me, so said hello again, to everyone. I sidled up behind them so they couldn't possibly miss me. They all just blanked me, like I was completely invisible. I just assumed that they didn't remember me.

I knocked on the department head's door and waited for him to call. He was sat behind his desk with his back to the window. And next to him was the University Director. As soon as I set eyes on him, I knew it wasn't going to be as straight forward as I'd hoped.

The department head gestured at the seat on the opposite side of his desk, the one nearest to me. As I was sitting, he turned to the director and they started talking about something, which sounded unrelated.

They kept me waiting for a minute or two, before they reached an agreement, signified by a short laugh. Then the department head made eye contact and said, "Dr Abu-Rgheff, how can I help you?"

I reminded him of our conversation in which he'd told me to come in, to discuss the prospect of my reinstatement.

The department head sniggered and said, "Dr Abu-Rgheff, I said nothing of the sort."

I protested. I'd spent the last two years protesting my innocence, and I was determined it wasn't going to continue. Especially when it involved people I'd previously thought of as my friends.

In the end, I managed to persuade them to give me my old job back. I sat back, let a smile cross my face and thanked them for their confidence in me. At that point, I felt proud of myself, the way I'd fought my corner and emerged victorious. I asked the department head when he wanted me to start.

The director answered for him. "Hang on a minute, don't go getting ahead of yourself. There is a proviso."

I couldn't imagine what this might be. I wasn't entirely sure he wasn't playing a joke on me. "What proviso?"

"We feel that your salary should be reviewed."

I still wasn't sure what he was talking about. The thought did occur to me that he was going to give me a reduced salary, but I quickly dismissed it as being unlikely. There were bound to have been increases due to inflation, so it was going to be a small pay rise.

"We feel that—your role isn't quite as vital to the running of the department as it was, and therefore, your recompense should be reduced accordingly."

I tried to think about the implications of this, shifting my priorities and making do rather than buying new. There was just one thing I needed to know, so I could make sense of it all. "How much are we talking about?"

His answer mortified me. All this time, I'd been thinking about getting back to normal and having money in my pocket. Now they were saying I'd be on the equivalent of a junior's pay. I wasn't finished yet, though. Maybe there was room for compromise. "OK, I know there have been changes, and my salary should be cut, but—"

This time the department head spoke up. "Those are the terms, Dr Abu-Rgheff, take it or leave it."

"Can I go home and think about it? I'm not sure if I can afford to live off that."

The department head produced a pile of papers from his drawer. "You see these? These are all from people, well-qualified people, that have applied for your job. A job that I've kept open for you for three years. Now, if you're telling me you're not sure—"

"OK, I'll take it."

My wife was supportive, just as I knew she would be. We stayed up talking well into the night. In the end, we concluded that things would be OK for the time being, provided she continued to work at the school. I went to bed, determined that my salary wasn't going to be reduced for long.

I'd just about managed to come to terms with my reduced salary by the time I started at the university, but things soon went from bad to worse.

I decided to forget about the way they'd all blanked me and try again to resume old friendships. However, as soon as I spoke, the reality of the situation hit home.

On one occasion, I went to say hello to a colleague that I'd known well. He was sat alone at his desk, going about his duties, with no distractions. However, he looked me in the eye and curled his lip, like he'd just seen something utterly distasteful. From that moment on, I knew that however much I tried, I was always going to be ostracised. I also decided that I'd come through too much to let this stand in my way, so I'd just do my job and go home to my family each night, without getting involved as I had done before.

We had to make cutbacks, far more significant than I'd first envisaged when they told me about my reduction in pay. I felt guilty for relying on my wife's wages the way I did, but we managed to get through with the support of my family.

At work, my salary was only part of the problem. A few months after my return, an opportunity arose for me to showcase my research at an overseas venue. This pleased me a lot and restored some of the self-confidence I'd lost while I was away.

This was a great coup for the university. They were always looking for ways to promote themselves and establish the university as a world-renowned facility.

I could hear the department head was on the phone as I approached the door to his office, so I stood waiting, thinking my moment to shine had come. This could even prompt them to restore my salary, meaning my family could have the things I wanted to give them

When he'd finished talking, I knocked on the door and waited for him to call.

"I have some fantastic news," I said, closing the door behind me.

He looked at me like he'd heard it all before. "What fantastic news?"

"There is an opportunity for me to travel overseas, to read out my research. Put the university back in the spotlight."

247

He said there were a few formalities to get out of the way first, adding that I should go and see the director.

The director's office was on the top floor, hidden away from the students. I felt like a naughty schoolboy going to see the headmaster.

The second my knuckles hit the door, he shouted for me to enter. He gestured for me to take the chair opposite him and continued with his reading, making me wait as long as he could. I'd say it was a good five minutes before he looked up to acknowledge me.

"Dr Abu-Rgheff, what can I do for you?"

I told him about the overseas conference and relayed to him what my department head had said.

"Yes, the *formalities*. I'm afraid there's a problem with your visa."

I was wise enough to know what was coming. "What kind of a problem?"

"The kind of problem that means you need Saddam's approval before you can leave the country."

Although I knew this was coming, it still came as a shock when he said it aloud. I left his office wondering what I had to do to restore my reputation.

I won't pretend the next few years were easy, but we got through them. My wife was very understanding and didn't so much as hint that she begrudged being the primary breadwinner.

Two years later, in 1985, our oldest daughter started at Hariri High School for Girls, and it was our youngest's turn to attend Muhheje Primary School. They went to my family house after school, where their grandma spoilt them until we collected them a few hours later. I got the feeling that my parents and children were both happy with the arrangement and didn't want those days to end.

Another year further on, my mother in law came to stay with us. Just like before, we had a great time. My wife managed to get some time off work, meaning they could be together constantly. When I got home, I noticed she looked happier than she had for a while, which endeared me to her mother even further. Most days, when our working day had finished, we all went out for a drive, the kids included.

Just before she left, we decided that sometime soon we'd make the trip to Yorkshire to visit her. She said it would be nice, but I could tell from the tone of her voice that she didn't think I was serious. This made me determined to keep my word.

As we travelled with her to the airport, I knew the last few weeks would be another precious memory that I'd reflect on later in life. None of us were getting any younger.

Around December time, 1986, I noticed my mum wasn't quite herself. I dismissed this at first as being a minor ailment, but as time passed, I became increasingly concerned. When I mentioned it to my sister, she suggested we take her to the doctors' straight away.

She'd never wholly recovered from her stroke in 1983. Although her walking had improved a lot, her slurred speech served as a constant reminder that something was wrong internally.

When my eldest brother took her to see the doctor, none of us saw it as a cause for concern. We were fully expecting her to return carrying a whole load of medicines, along with instructions for her to take things easy. However, the minute we clapped eyes on my brother, we knew we had underestimated the gravity of the situation.

The doctor was very worried. He'd said he hoped it would amount to nothing and her symptoms would go away by themselves, but he couldn't guarantee anything. He said to make another appointment in the New Year if things didn't improve.

She did get better over the following weeks. It was a magnificent New Year, with everyone together, enjoying themselves. My mum insisted on doing most of the cooking as she always did. There were a few accidents in the kitchen, but they could have happened to anyone.

As she'd improved so much, we assumed that she'd recovered as the doctor had hoped. In fact, she looked healthier than she had for years. It came as a great shock to us then when she woke up one morning, and the lights had gone out again. She got progressively worse over the next few days, so we took her back to the doctor. He delivered the verdict we'd all dreaded.

It took me a long time to get over my mother's death. Now I was on my own in the world, with no parents to look up to and offer guidance when I most needed it. I remember returning to my house after the wake. I dropped onto the sofa and cried my eyes out. My wife put her arm around me and tried to give me some comfort, but I could tell from the way she was snivelling that she felt just as devastated as I did.

The worst part of all was having to explain it to my daughters. My oldest understood and immersed herself in grief like the rest of us, but my youngest didn't know what was going on. She just kept asking why she couldn't go round to her grandma's anymore. My wife told her, but I'm not sure if it sunk in, not for a while anyway.

Everything felt strange without Mum, but we soon adapted. She will always be with us in our hearts.

Being a man of my word, in 1988 I applied for a visa for my family and I to visit my mother in law in the UK. The response I received wasn't wholly unexpected.

I could have either a visa for myself alone or one for my family to go without me. Saddam's intent was clear: he wanted to hold me or my family prisoner until the other came back. My wife decided that I should go alone.

My children thought it was strange that I'd broken my promise. I could see how upset they were when I told them that they wouldn't be seeing their grandma after all. They'd also been looking forward to meeting their relatives and making friends with their cousins. None of us wanted this to happen and it was a teary goodbye.

Despite the cold weather, I relished every minute of my time in the UK, and I was glad to have a respite from the intense summer heat of Baghdad.

On the plane home, I made plans for our next visit, when we'd hopefully be all together. If this couldn't happen, then it was the turn of my family

Dr Mosa Abu Rgheff

to make the trip   An alternative was for my mother in law stay with us and experience springtime in Baghdad.

This was one plan that never came to fruition.

Chapter 15

"Bye Mosa, see you tomorrow," I turned to wave at the university's receptionist on my way out. It was a typically hot summer's night. I smiled to myself at the way people in the UK make such a fuss whenever the temperature rises a few degrees above the norm. My wife had done very well to acclimatise; not many would.

It was roasting in my car. The leather seat baked my legs through my smart work trousers as I left the confines of the university car park and turned onto the main road.

Almost immediately, a white truck cut in front of me. I slammed on the breaks, and only just in time. I was in such a good mood that the driver of this vehicle didn't bother me in the least. I just nodded, focused on the road ahead and proceeded to drive home.

I was always in a happy mood when I'd just left work; who isn't? I usually remained in high spirits until half an hour or so after I'd eaten, when I remembered that I only had a few hours before bedtime. But that hot, June night, was one that I'd remember forever.

I felt especially happy. I was happy because my brother Hussein was home on leave from the army, and he was coming round later, just like in the old days. Well, not quite. My daughters were older now. They still looked forward to their uncle Hussein's visits, but it didn't excite them quite as much as it had. I thought back for a minute to the way they used to sit transfixed, their eyes sparkling in the fading daylight, as they listened to one of his stories. They were great days which, sadly, had gone forever.

My wife was waiting for me at the door, as was her custom. After catching up with the day's events, we ate and then sat down. Usually, Hussein came for dinner, but tonight he had some prior engagements with some of his army friends, so was visiting later in the evening.

As it approached Hussein's expected time of arrival, the conversation slowed until it stopped altogether. We were expecting him to open the back door and shout his greetings at any moment. Half an hour later, there was still no sign.

"He's late," my wife said, looking through the window."

She was right, but at that stage, I was only mildly concerned. Whilst this was out of character, he was a sociable fellow, and there was a good chance he'd got carried away with his friends and overlooked the time. So, I told my wife not to worry and that we'd hear the backdoor open at any minute.

My wife told the girls to hush, and we listened for the door in silence. The night was starting to draw in outside. The sun had almost sunk behind the distant hills and the outline of the moon was visible. I have to admit that it was a beautiful sunset, with its rays painting the landscape red. I spent a second or so admiring the view, before glancing up at the clock on the wall. Something must have happened to him.

We continued to sit for a while, trying to think of plausible reasons for his tardiness and therefore give ourselves some peace of mind. We'd just reached a consensus when the phone rang. The events of seven years previously played out in my mind, and my mouth went dry.

"Hello, Uncle Mosa." It was my niece. I took a deep breath and glanced at the ceiling to give my thanks to Allah.

"I have some bad news, Uncle Mosa."

I knew what was coming. Call it brotherly intuition if you like, but the moment she'd finished her sentence I knew. My voice trembled as I asked her what the news was.

"It's Hussein."

For some inexplicable reason, this appeased me somewhat. I'd gone jumping to conclusions before, most notably when my mother came round to tell me he'd been taken, back in 1981. That time, his arrest had come as a relief.

"What about him?"

Two minutes later, I was in my car, weaving my way around the traffic as I rushed to the hospital.

I turned onto the corridor leading to A&E and saw my siblings. Despite the empty seats in the waiting area, they were standing, reassuring one another and saying that everything was going to be OK. Despite this, my sister looked especially distraught as my older brother did his best to console her.

"Mosa," my sister cried as I entered the scene. She rushed over the pristine white floor to wrap her arms around me. She pressed her face into my chest and said Hussein was her best friend in the world. I patted the back of her head and said I felt precisely the same.

"Where is he?" I asked my older brother, who had assumed the responsibility of holding everyone together.

"He's being assessed," he replied, glancing over his shoulder at a room with the door closed, sealed off from the rest of the hospital. I stared through the door's darkened glass window, trying to look in through the mesh. I held my breath to try and hear what was going on behind the door, silently cursing everyone for being so noisy.

We sat on the seats in the waiting room, biting our nails, too nervous to talk. Despite all the surrounding noise, all I could hear was my sister sobbing, which in turn, brought tears to my own eyes.

Looking along the row of red, plastic chairs, I could tell that all of my siblings were trying to listen in on the room with the darkened glass, just as I was. My brother averted his gaze from the tiled floor and declared, without turning his head to look at us, that no news was good news.

It wasn't long after that, I'm not sure how long exactly, that the door opened. We all turned around as one to try and catch a glimpse of the doctor's face, looking for signs that Hussein had recovered. But there was nothing. Judging by the way he moved across the tiled floor, it looked like it could be bad news. So I was bracing myself for the worst when the doctor stood over my elder brother and asked him to follow him back into the room whence he'd come.

My brother obliged, leaving us to sit there in silence, holding our breath to try and hear something, anything, of what was being said. I silently cursed the woman sat nearest the door for occupying the seat that I most wanted.

The door opened, and my brother stepped out. He beckoned us all to gather round, which we did. The first thing he said produced a collective sigh of relief.

"The good news is that he's still fighting. His condition hasn't deteriorated much since the paramedics brought him in."

However, it wasn't long before my thoughts ventured beyond the perceived good news and scrutinised the intricacies of the sentence. He hadn't deteriorated, but we knew nothing of his condition when he was first brought in to A & E. This piece of information told us nothing, not really.

"There's a pretty big but, though," my brother continued, "the doctor also said the injuries were life-threatening. He said he wasn't sure how long he could hold on for, if at all."

It was at this moment that the gravity of the situation hit us all. Up until that point, we'd feared the worst, but there'd been this tiny sliver of hope. For all we knew, his vital organs could have been left in working order. If this was so, a full recovery was likely. Now, everything seemed so final.

My sister, who was stood beside me, burst into tears. I took hold of her hand to offer some comfort, but alas, there were no more reassurances to give.

Before we'd had the chance to fully absorb the news, the doctor appeared. He called a porter over and asked him to take us to a room where we could have a bit more privacy. We followed the porter through the waiting area, to a room with some comfortable seats and a small table. Once we were all seated, I tried to catch a glimpse of the world outside through the tiny gap at the top of the dark blue curtains. After a few moments of silent contemplation, my sister stood up and switched the light on. As soon as she'd returned to her seat, I asked my brother if Hussein was suffering.

My brother knew that above all, we wanted the truth. "I'm afraid so. The doctor said he's in severe pain."

This came as a great shock to everyone, even though it had been evident from the start. I think we'd all been trying to avoid thinking about it, and now it was official, it had been brought to the front of our minds. My sister started sobbing, but this time another of my siblings began to snivel too. Seeing my brother cry like that broke my own resolve.

We sat in silence for a while, too upset to talk, until my sister stood up and said it was getting late. She'd left her children in the care of a neighbour and didn't think it was fair on them to stay any later. We said farewell and gave her some parting solace. No sooner had the door shut then the silence returned.

The thought then occurred to me that Hussein might not survive the night, in which case, my sister would probably be beating herself up forevermore. I prayed that this wouldn't happen, if only for her sake.

I wasn't sure if my siblings were thinking the same thing, so I kept my thoughts to myself. I didn't want to go making things worse than they already were for everyone. Shortly, another of my siblings said he'd better be going too.

The door swung open and the doctor appeared. He patted my sibling on the back and said he'd do all he could to make sure Hussein made a full and healthy recovery. When our eyes met, I made a snap decision. "Doctor?"

I asked the consultant if I could see Hussein. He nodded and took me into the room where Hussein was laid, too weak to acknowledge my presence, fighting for his life. Seeing him like that, with a labyrinth of wires around him and a machine beeping at the arrival of each new second, the thought that he might not survive the night, resurfaced. I had no hesitation in asking the doctor if I could be with him.

The doctor said, of course it would be OK, but he would have to be moved from A & E into a ward. A

porter, the same one that had taken us to the private room, took hold of the metal railings and the wheels began to rotate in a reverse motion.

I followed the porter through a series of waiting rooms, and along a corridor to a ward. That's where the disinfectant smell that's common to all hospitals hit me for the first time. The porter had a short chat with the sister, and we proceeded on our way. Once we had passed through another two wards, all packed full of sick people in their pyjamas, we came to a halt. This time the sister nodded and pointed to a vacant slot. The porter inserted my brother between two elderly gentlemen and said goodbye.

I stood by Hussein's side, talking to him about our childhood, hoping he'd come round and murmur a reply, or at least open his eyes to acknowledge me. Then a group of male nurses told me to stand aside while they transferred him from one of the makeshift beds they use in A & E to a permanent ward bed. Once the transfer was complete, they brought me a chair. I took hold of Hussein's hand and sat down.

The wooden chair was hard. As concerned as I was about Hussein, I still had to keep on shifting from one buttock to the other. I heard talking at the ward's reception desk, followed by some authoritative sounding footsteps clapping on the tiled floor. He came to a halt at Hussein's bed and introduced himself as the ward doctor. After conducting a quick examination, he called the nurse and told her to have him transferred to intensive care.

After they'd parked the bed and connected him up to a flashing machine, I took hold of his hand again and continued to talk about our childhood. This time he opened his eyes and smiled at me.

I shouted the nurse, who came running over, worried that he'd taken a turn for the worst. She looked just as happy as I was to see his eyes open. She encouraged me to continue talking to him, which I did. I asked him over and over how he felt, but he was in too much pain to reply. When the nurse told me to let him rest, I left the ward, but I was determined not to leave him.

I laid on the floor outside the hospital and did my utmost to make myself comfortable for the night. It was cold and hard, and I knew my back would make me suffer in the morning, but I'd slept on worse; much worse.

Hospital carparks are just as busy at night as they are during the day. With the headlights shining in my face and all the coming and going, I gave up trying to sleep and sat up. I did think of going inside to see if I could find a snippet of news, but decided that would be pointless. Besides, as the receptionist pointed out, even if they did let me see him, I would only be a distraction. It was best to let the doctors and nurses go about their job unhindered.

As soon as it was light, I asked the receptionist about the visiting hours and made myself comfortable on a seat beside the hospital's rotating door. from where I watched the clock go round. I observed each tick of the second hand for roughly three hours, until a bell sounded and all the waiting friends and relatives poured in.

"You can see your brother now," the receptionist told me.

I'd only just arrived at the ward when there were footsteps, along with some voices that I knew well.

I smiled at my sister in law, who was heavily pregnant. She gave me a half-hearted smile in return. I stood back to let her see her husband, and then set about keeping her children occupied, for which I could tell she was grateful.

After a minute or so, she beckoned the children forward, and his family stood around his bed. His wife shrieked with joy when he opened his eyes and smiled at her. I watched him try to talk, but just like the night before, no words would come. He soon gave up and instead turned to look at his children. He smiled at each of them, but remained too weak to talk. It was a sad moment. If anyone was going to coax him into talking it was his children. I glanced at his wife, whom I could see was thinking the same thing as me.

Three days after he was first admitted, I went to visit for what would turn out to be the last time. I stood over him, took hold of his hand and did my best to take our minds off the dire situation in which we found ourselves. For a while, he did manage to perk up. His words were weak, and I had to strain to hear him. Still, he was talking and able to make the occasional contribution to the conversation.

We continued in the same vein for a while, until there came a natural break the conversation. As I stood listening to the beeps and watching the flashing lights through my periphery, my previously high spirits dissipated. My brother was in a very precarious position, and I shouldn't be exhausting him as much as I was. So, I insisted he get some rest. Waving away his protests, I sat on the chair beside his bed and told him I'd be there when he felt better.

He soon fell asleep. I waited, my eyes flitting from Hussein to the clock until, eventually, he stirred. He turned to check that I was still there. As soon as he saw me, he smiled and said hello. I smiled back and asked how he was feeling. He said he was better and that he had a small favour to ask of me.

I made the single step from the chair to his bedside, where I moved my ear towards his mouth.

It seemed to me his condition had deteriorated in the two minutes since he had awoken. He murmured my name, and I moved my head further towards his mouth, until I could feel his shallow breath on my ear.

I took hold of his hand and asked what he wanted me to do.

He asked me to tell one of our other siblings to assist his family in every way he could. I didn't like the way he seemed to be putting his affairs in order in preparation for his absence. He continued, asking me to ask our sibling to look after his children. He wanted him to make sure they received the best possible education, and they were always cared for. I smiled and said to leave everything to me. He soon fell asleep, at which point left him in peace. I knew it was just a matter of time.

When I arrived home, I tried not to convey my worries to my family and did my best to put a brave face on it for them. At night, I lay awake, comparing how he was a few months earlier to how weak and feeble he looked in his hospital bed.

Hussein died a few days later, on 28th June 1988. He left behind four children and a wife that was heavily pregnant with his child.

Chapter 16

I sat on the sofa, my eyes red and stinging. Through the window I studied the hills in the far-off distance. Although I couldn't see it from there, I knew there to be a farmhouse. I sat transfixed, wondering what they were doing on that day of all days and how it must feel to be oblivious of what had just happened to Hussein. I couldn't foresee how I would ever be able to come and go like them again. Not without feeling the burden of my younger brother's death every step of every journey I took.

I noticed the sun had climbed high into the sky, making me squint and roasting my face. I had no choice but to look away and divert my attention to the fireplace in front of me instead.

It was my daughters that freed me from my trance. They were talking loudly about something, although I could tell they were subdued. I made the short journey upstairs to sit with them on the bed. I had the urge to put my arms around them and tell them I wasn't ever letting go. I dropped on the bed and sat sandwiched in between them. We talked about the issues most important to them for half an hour or so, until the door opened, and my wife entered.

After ruffling up the girls' hair, she sat down beside my daughter, right at the end of the bed. She squeezed my hand and reminded me that there were preparations to make.

She was right. I sprung to my feet and descended the stairs, running straight to the chair beside the phone. I had a lot to do, and time was running out.

Islamic custom dictates that a body must be buried within 24 hours of death. The first thing on my agenda was to phone my siblings to find out what had been done already. Fortunately, my elder brother was responsible for making the arrangements and he had already got to work. Hence, everything was on schedule and there was no need to panic. I'd forgotten that the oldest sibling traditionally makes the arrangements. I felt grateful for this, but at the same time, sorry for my brother who had to shoulder the responsibility despite the inner turmoil he must be feeling himself. Not for the first time and by no means the last, I thanked Allah for giving me such a wonderful family.

It goes without saying that that night, the 28th June 1988, was among the worst of my life. I lay awake in bed, long after my wife had shut her eyes, comparing the current situation to the nights I spent in prison, and decided that the latter was preferable. I was wrong to say that night was among the worst of my life. No, it was the worst by a long way and that probably included when my parents had died, as they were old and had experienced far more of life.

At some point during the night, my wife awoke. Noticing that I was laid awake in the dark, she rubbed her eyes and asked if I had managed to get any sleep at all. I shook my head, prompting her to say she wasn't going to go back to sleep, because I needed her, and I had a long day ahead. I insisted that she close her eyes, adding that there was little point in us both suffering from sleep deprivation. I asked her more than once, but that didn't prevent her from staying awake so she could give me the support she said I needed.

Early the next morning, my wife, my daughters and I made the short journey to the family house, to wait for Hussein's body. When it arrived, my sister screamed, "no" and retched, as if she was going to be sick. Although I didn't show it, I knew exactly how she felt. We then waited in silence for the hearse to arrive, which felt like hours, but was no more than half an hour.

Hussein's wife and children made the short trip to the cemetery in the car immediately behind the hearse, with myself and my siblings following them. Behind us, came our outer family and Hussein's friends. It was a big precession, which was only to be expected for such a likeable and sociable person.

We were heading for the family cemetery, which was located in an area called Najaf, just south of Baghdad.

With my eyes firmly focused on the car in front, which was nothing more than a teary blur, I noticed in my periphery, pedestrians stopping to honour the deceased. This is another long-standing tradition that forms part of all Islamic funerals.

We followed the cars in front into the cemetery and I watched Hussein's wife leave her car, dabbing her eyes with a white tissue. As more people arrived, a queue formed as everyone waited for their turn to pray over Hussein's body, which is done according to Islamic rules.

A car came to a halt outside the cemetery gates, and a man got out. He looked like he was approximately the same age as my elder brother. He wore a black suit and walked with the sombre demeanour of a chief mourner. Hussein's wife turned to see from whence the footsteps came and gave the man a smile.

He extended his hand and expressed his condolences, the same as everyone else. There

277

was just something about him that gave everyone an extra shot of emotion, which was expressed in the form of tears. Hussein's wife was the worst hit. She looked down at the grass on which she stood and released a shower of teardrops, before extracting a fresh tissue from her top pocket and wiping her eyes.

The man, as it turned out, had been charged with the preparation of Hussein's grave. He had just wanted to introduce himself to Hussein's wife, so she could put a face to him. I turned to watch him get back into his car and embark on the short journey to the plot that had been allocated to Hussein.

For a minute, despite the size of the gathering, all we could hear were birds singing, leaves rustling in the breeze and the distant rumble of a car engine. I stood in silent contemplation, thinking about all the good times I'd had with Hussein, trying to come to terms with the fact that I wouldn't be seeing him again. I tried to push the image I had of him lying in the hospital bed to the back of my mind, and instead focus on the young, friendly man that I had grown up with. Finally, it was the sound of someone, probably his wife, sobbing that returned my thoughts to the here and now. I had to remain stoic, to try and be strong for all those around me. However, I feared the outpouring of grief I'd feel later that night when I was alone with my wife and my daughters had gone to bed.

I decided to visit the grave. I had been very close to my brother, closer than I was to any of my other siblings, and I felt the need to say goodbye alone so that I could share more of our memories. So, I informed my wife of my intentions, in response to which she nodded and said to take as long as I needed.

To my surprise and annoyance, I wasn't the only person stood at the grave. There was a young man, of a similar age to Hussein.

I sidled up to the man said hello. Judging by the informal way with which he spoke about Hussein, he must have been a close friend. Perhaps someone Hussein had known from the army. His wife had been responsible for that side of things. I introduced myself as Hussein's older brother, in the hope that he'd reciprocate, without being prompted. The stranger obliged and confirmed that he was a friend. Someone Hussein had known for a good few years, which made me feel slightly guilty for not recognising him.

He commented that the circumstances surrounding Hussein's death were unjust. I agreed and told him about Hussein's earlier experiences, which he knew nothing of. I then lowered my head to look at the grave, thus bringing an end to the conversation. The man took the hint and left the scene.

Now all alone, I shielded my eyes from the mid-day sun and focused on the grave. There were so many things I wanted to say, plans that I had for us both that we never got round to doing. I had talked to him at length about our childhood in the hospital, so now I wanted to focus on the rest of our lives

Things like his evening visits after work and his stories which had held my daughters spellbound. Also, memories of his wedding, and mine. All the things that were private to us both, that no one else knew about. I went there intending to say all these things, but now, when

I was alone and had the perfect opportunity, the words wouldn't come.

As I stood overlooking the grave, pain numbed my mind. I tried to compose myself and force some thoughts from my head to my mouth, but they had faded away into the distance. The only thing I was aware of was sound of my tears pattering against the ground.

My mind awoke and started taking a course of its own, like it was a wholly sinister external entity that was separate from the rest of my body. My thoughts went back to our childhood and then jumped forwards through time, creating a mental image of all the significant phases of our lives.

This wasn't a pleasant experience, more like torture beyond anything I'd ever endured or been witness to. Then, for the grand finale, the alien being inside my head seized hold of my rational thoughts and played the cruellest of tricks on me

For a split second, I forgot that he was there, in the box buried in the ground. I smiled and decided I'd share a few memories with him when I got home and tell him how much I cared about him. Then I regained control of my thoughts and released a second flood of tears onto his grave.

A car pulled up and someone got out. It was time to let someone else have their turn, so I walked away and left him in peace.

When I joined the others, my wife came running over and said she was starting to get worried about me. I apologised and scanned the crowd of people, looking for my siblings. I just wanted to make sure they were OK and were coping with the emotional turmoil. I was pleased to see they were all well, deep in discussion with various relatives that none of us had seen for many years. Funerals and wedding always bring people together and strengthen bonds that had frayed.

My older brother, who had done a great job so far called for everyone's attention and announced it was time to go back to our family home for the wake.

Hussein's wife and children were there already. His wife was stood at the door, welcoming everyone as they entered. She was doing her best to put on a brave face, but her bloodshot eyes told everyone that she'd cried herself dry. I said hello as I passed and she squeezed my arm, making an exception of me. I turned to give her a smile, in response to which she lowered her voice and said we'd get through it together. Something then compelled me to say hello to his children and promise them a trip out when their mum was feeling up to it. This made them smile, which in turn brought a flicker of a smile to their mother's face.

Once everyone was inside, Hussein's wife went into the kitchen to collect the food that she'd prepared earlier. All the immediate family went to help her. I have to say that again she'd done a great job, which my wife also noticed.

When everyone had had their fill, we all went out into the garden. A large tent had been assembled for the Al-Fatihah[1], which, traditionally, is disassembled after three days.

---

[1] Al Fatihah word itself is the name of the first surah in the Quran. This could be interpreted as the preface of the holy book. It is generally hinted at introduction / preparation for what follows.

Fatihah is an essential part of a funeral; it suggests the beginning of life after death. Surrat Al-Fatihah also announces usually loudly in wedding events for blessing the start of the marriage's life. It is imperative in Islam that the family of the deceased wear black and men wear black shirts or

Hussein's Fatihah was attended by his friends, relatives and siblings.

The women went into the house and left the men to enter the tent. The women cooked dinner whilst they shared memories of Hussein's life. It was a very emotional affair, in which many tears were shed.

I joined the back of the queue leading to the tent, as I struggled to prevent my mind from diverting to memories of Hussein once again. This was a new beginning for him. He was now saying goodbye to a world that was dominated by the rich and evil and entering heaven, to be rewarded for his faith. It was an occasion to be happy, but that did nothing to take away the mind-numbing pain my siblings and I were feeling. It is fair to say that I had somewhat conflicting emotions.

On entering the tent, I shouted, "Al-Fatihah," as I made my way towards a seat that my siblings had saved for me.

---

ties. The Fatihah continues for three consecutive days. The family and relatives of the deceased must visit his resting place 40 days after death.

Once the process was complete, I rose up and smiled at my siblings. We each shouted, "Al-Fatihah", as we left the tent and stepped outside onto the garden.

Back in the house, the women had finished cooking and now it was the turn of my siblings and I to serve the traditional selection of cooked meats and make the guest feel welcome.

Hussein's wife had once again done him proud with the food. He'd have been eating it with relish if he was there. I thought of him devouring the fantastic food that had been made in his honour and for the first time that day managed to muster up a smile.

The food was just for the guests and the elder of the family, who was my oldest sibling. I whispered the protocol to my wife and informed her that it was time to leave. On our way out of the family house, it was my wife's turn to shout, "Al-Fatihah."

With the ceremony complete, we headed back to our own house, where we prepared our own meal and ate it with our daughters.

After we'd eaten, I dropped onto the sofa and enjoyed a moment's silent solitude whilst my wife attended to our daughters. Later on, when my wife and I were alone, we reflected on the day's events and formed the consensus that it went as well as anyone could have wished for.

My wife asked me about earlier in the day, when I went to see Hussein's grave, and the sombreness returned. I felt a lump form in my throat. A minute or so later, tears welled up in my eyes. My wife noticed and reached across the sofa to take hold of my hand. Seeing the love in her eyes and how deeply she cared for me, I broke down and wept.

She tried to make things better by changing the subject and then went into the kitchen to make us both a drink. When she came back, I had stopped crying and she was wearing a smile. We started talking about other things, mostly our daughters, but my siblings and her mother came up too. This helped no on end, and by the time I went to bed, I was feeling better than I had all day.

As soon as the lights went out, though, I couldn't help but go over and over the events of the day. I tried my hardest not to torture myself by thinking about all the good times I'd shared with Hussein. I succeeded in doing this, but at a cost. Instead, my train of thought journeyed towards the time I'd spent alone with Hussein at his grave and the man that claimed to be his friend. I racked my brain to try and put a name to his face, but I couldn't recollect anything, which again led me to surmise that maybe he wasn't who he said he was. I was too tired to give this the thought it required and soon found myself drifting off to sleep.

When I awoke, the sun was shining through the gap at the top of the curtains, creating a patch of light on the sheet beside me. I looked over my shoulder to discover that I was alone. Given everything that had gone on, my first instinct was to panic and thoughts ran through my mind that maybe she'd been arrested during the night and taken away. When I heard her chastising my daughters over something and nothing, I breathed a sigh of relief and smiled as I sat up.

I soon determined that she was cleaning the house in preparation for me getting up. The clock beside me said that I'd slept well, so she'd probably got up earlier, quiet as a mouse.

Just as I'd thought, my wife had been hard at work with the cleaning, and what's more, she'd made a delicious breakfast. She'd done her very best to make me feel better and she'd succeeded. Despite my loss, I still had my own family, which I adored and who adored me.

As my wife cleared the dishes and started on the washing up, my mind flashed back to the man at the grave. I tried again and again to place him and became increasingly apprehensive as I continued to fail. My wife noticed my distant expression and asked what was troubling me, adding that she could tell it wasn't Hussein, not this time.

So I told her about the man I saw at the grave and said I was worried that he might have been trying to hide something. She shook her head reassuringly and asked me to recount the scene in its entirety. I did this without mentioning the part when my mind went blank.

Once I'd finished, my wife said something that took me entirely by surprise. She asked me again what he'd said when we first met, and I responded.

Then she pointed out that if he said it was unjust, then maybe he knew something. And she had a point.

Chapter 17

They say time is a great healer, but whenever I think my dear brother Hussein, I still break out into tears.

It might come as no surprise then, that the next week or so is memorable for all the wrong reasons. I spent the days following the funeral at home with my wife, and then it was weekend. On the Sunday afternoon, I started thinking about going back to work, so I mentioned it to my wife. She said it might be a good idea, as it would help to take my mind off things for nine hours a day, five days a week.

So that's what I did, but it didn't make things any easier, not at first and not by a long shot. I remember how, when I first stepped into my office, everyone greeted me with a smile. Whilst I nodded back in acknowledgement, it just felt like I was observing them through a cloud, from where the everyday chit-chat felt so meaningless it was irritating.

The items on my desk were no different. My pen, phone, note pad, all my research; they were just reminders. Reminders of the Friday night not so long ago, when I lived in an entirely different world. The worst thing of all was my pen. The moment it inserted itself between my thumb and fingers, I told myself that the last time I touched this long, slender object, Hussein was alive. I dropped it on my desk and sat back as it clattered, like the pen was responsible for all my problems.

A colleague came over to ask me a work-related question. Trying to remain professional, and not to let my circumstances affect my job performance, I gave him a precise and succinct answer, which answered his query and then some. He then made the ill-judged comment that

I looked like I needed cheering up, so he pulled out a chair and sat at the opposite side of my desk.

To begin with, I found his small talk irritating and wished he'd go away and leave me in peace. But then, gradually, I started to engage with him. This short encounter brought me back to the land of the living, and it was due to this that I was able to get through the rest of the morning.

Whilst going back to work didn't take my mind of Hussein, I worried that I would make mistakes and be reprimanded by a boss that was ignorant to my situation, which did shift my thinking towards the bigger picture. More specifically, how and why he was killed. Once that thought had surfaced, it took over my mind and wouldn't give me a minute's peace until my questions were answered

I went to bed that night, confident I could get some sleep, but after several hours of lying awake, trying to work things out, I crept out of bed to sit in the kitchen. I needed to clarify what I knew already, and give more thought to the theory that had been running around my head since the moment I had woken the previous day. I had to do this before I could get some sleep.

The first thing I did was glance at the clock on the kitchen wall, which read just after **4.15** am. I couldn't believe I was up at this time, what with work in the morning. My eyes stung with tiredness, but I knew this silent contemplation was necessary if I was going to get any sleep at all.

I began by attempting to clarify the questions that had been posed in part by the man I saw at the grave, the one that claimed to be Hussein's friend. I had believed him in the immediate aftermath, but as time had progressed, I had become increasingly sceptical. Once I'd shed some light on this, I could then work my way backwards and uncover the gaps in the story that needed filling.

The trouble was that my mind was so tired and clouded that I couldn't think clearly, so I went into the living room to fetch a pen and notepad from the cupboard. My daughters always had sundries like this lying around.

The chairs in the kitchen were hard, and, despite the time of year, there was a definite chill. That, combined with my tired state of mind, made my writing virtually illegible, but as the notes were for my eyes only, this didn't really matter.

The most urgent questions, those that had caused me to lie awake half the night, were why Hussein was killed and who was the assassin. I needed to know if he had been singled out or if this was just a mindless act of brutality, carried out by a young tearaway, looking to impress his friends. Anything was possible, although I considered some theories to be more probable than others

Hussein was not a violent person. He had many friends in the community and no political opinions that might cause the authorities to become agitated. However, this hadn't stopped them from taking him back in 1981.

I gave much thought to the possibility that he was targeted, eventually deciding that there was not enough evidence to form a conclusion.

I didn't want to go back to bed with even more questions floating around than there had been when I got up. So I focused my mind on the how rather than the why. Hussein's wife must surely be able to give me some answers, but it might be too soon. There was the police inquest too, but we hadn't heard back from them with any findings. So, I had the choice of sitting around on my hands or at least making an attempt to talk to his wife.

The birds started singing outside. I'd been there quite some time so decided, since I'd made a small amount of progress, to return to bed and try to get in a couple of hours' sleep before I had to get up for work.

Needless to say, I was both tired and distracted the following day, but I don't think my performance was affected. I hadn't had opportunity to talk to my wife that morning, so one of the first questions she asked me when I got home was why I got up in the middle of the night. I explained to her the reason and my intended course of action.

To begin with, she wasn't sure that it was a good idea to approach Hussein's wife so soon after the funeral. My wife reminded me that she was still in grieving and might not be ready to talk about it just yet.

However, after further consideration, she changed her opinion. She said that the cathartic effect of getting it off her chest might actually do some good, adding that she'd phone Hussein's wife to try and determine the situation so she could advise me properly.

I let the subject drop so that I could spend the rest of the evening enjoying the company of my family.

I returned home the following evening to find my wife on the phone. She smiled at me and waved, which I understood to mean sit down on the sofa and wait for her to finish the conversation. It was obviously Hussein's wife on the other end of the line.

My wife thought it would be OK to visit her that evening, so that's what I did, straight after I'd eaten. As soon as I set eyes on her though, I felt it might have been a mistake, and she wouldn't be ready to entertain any visitors for the foreseeable future.

I felt grateful to my wife for paving the way, as otherwise I'd have turned around and gone straight back home. I told her to start right from the beginning and spare me no details. In response, she nodded and readied herself.

Right away, she gave me new information, something I couldn't possibly have known.

She said Hussein was at home one day, having a rest. He must have been tired, because he'd started to doze off, which he hardly ever did. His wife had gone outside and noticed a neighbour running across the street to talk to her. She couldn't think what it might be, so was curious to find out what she had to say.

Struggling to recover her breath, the woman said that Hussein's best friend had been shot.

I couldn't believe what I was hearing, but it did hint at what might have happened. This was just a theory I had, though, which need a lot more evidence before I could afford it any kind of credibility.

Once she'd calmed down some, the neighbour told Hussein's wife that the body had just been brought home. Having said all she'd had to say, so she walked home, leaving Hussein's wife to relay the news to my brother.

She struggled to continue. I squeezed her hand and said she'd done well to tell me this much and we'd continue another day. She shook her head and said it was something that had to be done.

She said that Hussein went to the door to see what he could find out. Then she stopped and went into her shell.

I didn't think it was fair to persist, so I got up and drove home. My wife said I'd done the right thing and I should let it drop for a while.

My wife was right to say I shouldn't go bothering Hussein's wife again, but I couldn't let it drop, if only for my own peace of mind. I had to get to the bottom of how it happened before I could solve the conundrum of why it happened. I had an idea.

Straight after work on the fifth day of that first week, I attended Friday prayers, which was as much about socialising as it was about giving thanks to Allah. I made sure I was the last to enter, so I could watch from a distance for the man that I saw at the grave. When this drew a blank, I went into the Mosque to pray. Afterwards, I walked briskly outside, trying to remain inconspicuous. It wouldn't have looked good if I was seen to be the last to enter and the first to leave.

Although there was no sign of the man himself, I did spot one of Hussein's other friends, whom I'd seen at the funeral. I fought my way through the crowd of people to talk to him.

There was no need to introduce myself, as he recognised me straight away. He was happy to see me, and we both got a bit emotional. As he turned to go on his way, I asked him for a favour.

"Do you know anything, about what happened to Hussein?"

The man shook his head. "I wish I did. I assume you've tried asking his wife. She was at the scene."

I told him that I'd been to see her already and she'd been helpful, but it was too traumatic for her to continue. He said he understood. I then asked him if there was anyone else who might know.

"Not that I know of, friend."

"I saw a man when I went to pay my respects at the graveside. He appeared to know him, or at least know how it happened." I described the man to him as best I could, but my recollection was fuzzy.

Hussein's friend shook his head. "Sorry, but he doesn't ring any bells. I wish I could help you, but—have you tried his old army unit?"

"No, not yet. I thought he might be an army friend, but I decided to try here first."

He wished me luck, and we parted company.

Driving towards Hussein's old army unit, I felt an overwhelming sense of déjà vu. I hadn't been down this way since he was arrested and taken over seven years earlier, in 1981. I wished I could have gone there under happier circumstances at least once in the intervening years.

Dr Mosa Abu Rgheff

I approached the reception tentatively, and I waited for the commanding officer to look up from his papers and grunt at me. The commander didn't like to be disturbed, least of all by a civilian. As soon as I opened my mouth, I knew it was going to be a thankless task. And so it turned out. With the benefit of hindsight, this was something I should have expected.

He just shrugged and said my description made no sense. And even if it did, there were thousands of candidates, so how was he to know who was right and who was wrong?

Not wanting to push my luck any further, I turned to face the door, my mind already trying to devise a plan C.

With one foot through the door, someone at the back of a group of soldiers that had just emerged from the mess caught my eye. I thought back to the man at the graveside, trying to compare the soldier in my periphery to the image I had in my head. By the time I looked again, he'd gone.

Another group of soldiers left the mess, one of whom looked at me and scowled. I'd obviously

302

overstayed my welcome. So reluctantly, I turned around and left the premises.

I wasn't ready to give up, though, not just yet. Once I was sat in the driver's seat of my car, I rested my forehead on the steering wheel. I put all the effort I could muster into formulating an alternative course of action. Nothing came to mind, nothing at all. I decided that if I talked it over with my wife, we might be able to come up with an alternative course of action between us, so I started up the engine to head for home.

However, no sooner had my indicator started to tick, then a soldier stepped out in front of me. I looked through the window to tell him to mind where he was going. He turned to glare at me. In the end, it was him that recognised me. I asked if he could spare five minutes of his time.

"Sure," he said, climbing into the passenger seat.

I glanced past him at the busy street and told him to close the door, before lowering my voice and asking about Hussein.

He confirmed that they'd served together, but offered no further information.

"Where you there, the day he was killed?"

"Yes, I was." He shook his head, his sorrow written all over his face.

I placed my hand on his shoulder and told him it was OK before I went on. "Can you tell me what happened?"

The man looked surprised. "What, don't you know?"

"Afraid not. I tried to ask his wife, but she's not quite up to it. The thing is, I really need to know. I need to get to the bottom of it."

The man nodded. "Of course you do, friend. It happened like this... "

Hussein, who was holding his young son, opened the door, just as a large and rowdy crowd had situated themselves outside his house.

They were very angry about something and were even firing a few bullets. For a second, Hussein stood still, trying to ascertain the cause of the commotion whilst acting as sentry to his house.

Then, without warning, a bullet pinged through the air and hit Hussein in his chest.

"Could it have been a stray bullet, do you think?"

The man shook his head. "No, I don't think so. They marched away straight afterwards, like their mission had been accomplished."

I couldn't believe that Hussein had died like that, in front of his family. I thanked the man as he unsettled himself, and again, just before he closed the door from the outside. Now I knew how it happened, I was in a position to try and find out why.

The minute I stepped through the front door, my wife could see that a weight had been lifted from me. She asked me what the man had told me and then said she was as shocked as me. When I informed her of my further intentions, she advised against it. She said I'd been through a lot and I needed some time to recover before I go raking up the past. As always, she was right.

So, I left it for a few weeks, to try and straighten things out in my own mind, before I went asking questions. I had a theory that Hussein had been targeted, possibly by the same people that had taken him in 1981. So, it was with this in mind, that I went to enquire at the local police station.

There had been an inquest into Hussein's death. The fact that the officer in charge had not received any information came as no surprise at all. He told me they might have some information at the main head office and to try enquiring there.

It took me a few days to consider if I would be wasting my time or not. I decided that I probably would be, but I had nothing to lose by trying. I thought it would be better to phone than go there in person.

When I made the call, they kept me waiting for as long as they could and then told me they'd had no involvement in the inquiry. They said I should go back to my local police station. I knew then that I was wasting my time for sure, but I had to try anyway.

I went back to the police station again and again, trying to persuade them to reopen the inquest. I argued that any homicide that included murder should be investigated. I also asked them to justify their decision not to take into consideration the human rights of the deceased.

No one made any attempt to listen. They just brushed it off or passed the buck on to someone else. In the end, there was no government investigation. I was left to conclude that Hussein could have been a target of the secret state police.

Chapter 18

1990

When the war with Iran ended, everyone felt as if they'd been freed of a huge burden. Although there wasn't any singing and dancing in the streets, inside, all my friends, neighbours, family and colleagues were delirious.

A couple of weeks later, when things were starting to return to normal, the soldiers began returning home. For a while, it seemed that everywhere I looked, I saw someone in uniform.

On one occasion, I saw a couple of officers walking along a neighbouring street. They were roughly the same age as Hussein would have been. I stopped to think of him for a moment, which brought tears to my eyes.

After a few months, the way of life that we'd become accustomed to started to change. Restrictions were removed, and we noticed then that media coverage shifted away from the military and gave more coverage to local issues. It was just like it had been in the 1970s.

I'm not sure when it happened exactly, but shortly after the new way of life became the norm, rumours started to surface of a possible lift in travel restrictions. None of us paid much attention to start with, as this was something we'd been promised many times before. Then I arrived home from work one night and noticed a newspaper beside the sofa, where my wife had been sitting. It was folded at a page with a headline confirming that this time the restrictions had been lifted. It was later, after we'd eaten, that my wife and I first had the conversation.

We hadn't been away as a family for a long time. So long ago that the memory had become faded with age, like a black and white picture in a book with yellow-tinged paper. There were many options. The conversation turned to possible holiday destinations, then I mentioned that I hadn't been to the UK for a while. My wife smiled and said we could take the opportunity to go and visit her brother in Baildon. With the destination settled, attention turned to our visa applications.

I remember sitting at the kitchen table, filling out the forms. My wife had been out earlier to buy some envelopes and had already paid the postage. All we had to do now was put our signatures to the documents, put them in the envelopes and take them to the post box. It all seemed so simple, and, looking at the excited faces all around me, my family had no doubts that everything would go according to plan. There was no reason to think our applications wouldn't be approved, but I wasn't convinced. I wouldn't believe it until I was holding them up in front of me. There was a chance that there'd be a catch, and I'd have to read the small print over and over before I felt able to invest all my trust.

Dr Mosa Abu Rgheff

We all went together to post the applications and then returned home, feeling happier than we had for a good while. I decided not to let my scepticism scupper their high spirits, so said nothing.

As time went by, without a hint of a reply, I started thinking about how I was going to break it to my daughters that it had all been a propaganda stunt. I had to find a way of keeping their disappointment to a minimum. Then there was my wife. Although I knew she wouldn't make a huge fuss if the applications were rejected, she'd be disappointed inside. I'd have to find a way of making her feel better too. I was clinging onto a slender hope that it wouldn't come to this, though.

I'd just about given up on the idea and was starting to think again about how I was going to tell my daughters, when I came home to find my wife holding four white envelopes. Smiling from ear to ear, she handed them to me. Everyone gathered round to watch me tear them open and extract their contents one by one. I placed them

312

on the table, before raising the first one up to the light.   When I'd read the front, I turned the document over to scan the small print.

I wished I was able to give the small print the attention it required there and then. The last thing I wanted to do was to build their hopes up, only to have them dashed later on when I 'd found the proviso or catch hidden away. But there was no opportunity to do this, so I had no choice but to take the risk.   I told my oldest daughter her application had been successful, hoping my wife wouldn't pick up on my apprehension.

My daughter screamed with delight. I could see my wife didn't think there was any cause for concern, and I had no reason to doubt her intuition. I tried to share in their excitement, but I couldn't, not just yet. So later on, when I was on my own, I took the opportunity to examine each and every word. It was only once I'd read and reread the small print that I held the visas up and allowed a smile to spread across my face. We were going to the UK.

From that moment on, I felt almost as excited as everyone else. We all sat down to discuss the finer points.   Deciding on the best time to go wasn't as easy as you might think, what with work and school.   In the end, we somehow managed to agree on a date that worked out well for each of us.

The following day, we telephoned the airline. They had a flight on the day we wanted, and there were four adjacent seats available.   For once, everything was going according to plan, without any glitches.

All that remained to do was to clear things at work, which I knew would be little more than a formality. I notified my colleagues and stayed a bit later each night, to make sure I didn't have too much of a backlog when I returned. Knowing me as well as she does, my wife not only understood, but she said she was fully expecting me to do this.

On the morning of 1ˢᵗ July 1990, we made the short journey to the airport. I didn't look back at my street, not once, nor did I at the university as we passed. At this stage, I honestly believed I'd be back at work, refreshed and raring to go, in a few weeks' time.   It's funny how things rarely turn out exactly how you expect them to.

There were one or two English people on the flight, businessmen and diplomats I expect. I could hear them talking about the weather and saying they were looking forward to getting back to the British climate. I smiled to myself, knowing full well that they'd change their tune once we landed at Heathrow in a few hours' time.

I knew when we were approaching the UK long before it was announced, because my wife began rubbing her shoulders and saying that it had turned chilly. Little under an hour later, the PA crackled, and the pilot made it known that we were approaching Heathrow. He added that it was an unusually hot summer and the UK was in the middle of a heatwave.

Everywhere I looked, there was only one topic of conversation. The newspapers, front and back were full of it. Unbeknown to me, I'd chosen to visit the UK in the middle of a football world cup. That night England were playing Cameroon in the quarter-finals.

We found a bench outside the airport, where we sat whilst we waited for our taxi. I noticed a man walk past with a stack of cases on a trolley.

I'd seen him on the plane and hadn't imagined that he'd have such quality, leather luggage. It made me look down at our luggage that I'd placed by our feet. We didn't have much to our name; just a few clothes and £1000. If we were going to make it last, we'd have to do things on a budget.

Baildon is a few hours' journey from London. We'd reserved seats on a train that would take us directly from Paddington to Leeds, where we'd booked another taxi to take us to Baildon.

On the train, everyone was too busy talking about the football to notice us, which gave us a chance to watch the scenery gradually change without being disturbed.

It was much cooler in Leeds than it had been in London. Nothing much had changed since I'd first lived there all those years earlier when I studied at the university. Everyone had the same gruff accent, but I knew they were friendly underneath. No sooner had we left the confines of the station car park and turned on to the main road, then the driver asked me if I'd heard about the football. When we stopped at some lights, he looked over his shoulder to face me. I could see the nervousness written all over his face. English people take this kind of thing far too seriously.

The minute the taxi pulled up outside my brother in law's house, the front door opened, and he came running out to greet us. He hugged my wife and then made a huge fuss of our daughters.

We went inside and had a cup of tea before we started unpacking. Later on, once we'd put our things away in the wardrobe we'd been allocated, we spent the rest of the night talking about possible plans for our stay. I could tell from my brother in law's face and from his excited chatter, that he'd been looking forward to seeing us as much as we had her.

It's safe to say that we all had a great time for those first few weeks. We went out more or less every day, exploring the local countryside and catching up with my wife's relatives that we hadn't seen for years. My daughters got on very well with their cousins, and so once or twice, we went out together, as one big family.

Then one day, at the start of August, I was sat conversing with my brother in law, when my wife thundered up the stairs. "What is it?" I asked as she entered the room.

Her next sentence winded me, like I'd been punched in the stomach.

"It's Saddam Hussein."

I knew full well that this was serious. "What about him, my dear?"

"He's started a new war. With Kuwait."

This brought the holiday phase of our stay to an abrupt and unwanted end. We spent most of the day watching the BBC for updates. We knew there were going to be implications for us, but we weren't quite sure what they'd be. As time passed, we became more and more worried for our safety. Roughly two weeks into the war, my wife said that it wasn't safe to go back with our daughters.

It seemed I'd been right all along. As soon as we'd decided to go on the trip, I'd been worrying, waiting for something to go wrong. I'd gone and made the mistake of thinking that we were going to be OK once we had our visas and we'd left Iraqi border control, but I'd been wrong. Saddam could still control our lives from afar.

Once my wife had finished talking, the true extent of our problems became apparent to me. She was right, of course. If our daughters couldn't go back, then neither could we. We'd all but spent the £1000 we'd arrived with, and we couldn't rely on my in-laws' generosity for much longer, not with our daughters to keep as well. No, one of us had to get a job, and I was determined that it wasn't going to be my wife. Besides that, we were all living together in a solitary bedroom. The situation wasn't ideal, and, if we were going to be staying for a prolonged period, this had to be addressed too. So it was decided that I would look for a job right away and then we'd find somewhere more suitable to live.

I racked my brains, trying to think of possible contacts that I could call upon in our hour of need. Then my wife suggested that I try at the university, which I thought was a great idea. I did some quick research and discovered that I needed to see Professor Howson. So I phoned the university and made an appointment.

I found the professor to be a very approachable and down to earth man. He put me at ease right away and then offered me a seat. I could see the university's grounds through the window over his shoulder.

With all the pleasantries out of the way, he asked me what he could do for me. I explained the situation and hoped for the best.

"It's a bad situation, back home in Iraq. I'm sure you've heard about the invasion of Kuwait?"

Professor Howson nodded and confirmed that he had, adding that he hoped Saddam would see sense and it wouldn't last all that long.

"I hope that is the case. But, knowing Saddam the way I do, I just can't see it."

The professor waved a hand. "You know better than me, I'm sure."

I then went on to explain how this had impacted my family and I. "I've had some bad experiences with the regime over the years." I swallowed before continuing. "They shot my brother. And now, as a consequence—I just don't trust him. I don't think it's safe for me to return with my daughters. "

"Absolutely. I agree one hundred per cent. Have you tried applying for asylum?"

This was something I had thought about, many times. I just didn't feel it was the right thing for me to do at that moment in time. I had no choice but to continue with my present course and ask if there was any chance of employment. He'd been accommodating so far, but I didn't want to push my luck.

"Well, I did think about this, but decided, well— I just don't think it's right for us at this time."

The professor understood. "That's fair enough. If it's not right for you, it's not right for you. What have you been doing so far?

I told him that we'd been staying with my brother in law. "It was OK at first, but it's a bit cramped, and besides, we're starting to run out of money."

"Oh, I see."

"So, with this in mind, I was wondering if there is anything available here, at the university?"

"At the university?" He paused to give it a moment's thought. "Well, there was—what exactly did you have in mind?"

"I could make a contribution to the department, by way of teaching or research."

"Well, in principle . . ." He paused for a minute or two to give the matter more thought. I could see the cogs turning in his mind through his shifting facial expressions. "Well, OK then. What would you say if I offered you a temporary contract?"

"For how long?"

"For one year."

I wasn't ideal, but I didn't want to appear ungrateful. "Yes, that's fine. What would you want me to do, Professor Howson?"

"I was thinking you could teach in our MSc programme. With some undergraduate supervision, and a research project too."

This sounded like just the kind of thing I'd been looking for. It's just a shame it was marred by the temporary contract. I would have like to do this long term, that's for sure.

I enjoyed my time at the university. It had been a while since I'd worked with young people and I relished the opportunity to do so again. Besides, last time it had been tainted by the way I kept on hearing about their deaths, one after the other. This was an experience I never wanted to go through again.

However, it was continually praying on my mind that I had a temporary contract, and, because of this I couldn't really settle. Although the money was useful, I didn't want to commit to more permanent accommodation unless my job was permanent too. So with this in mind, I had to continue with my job search whilst I was in employment, and not leave it until it was too late.

I looked long and hard for a permanent academic position, but I couldn't find anything. I had just about given up and was about to resort to asking Professor Howson for a contract extension, when I found an opening at the University of Plymouth.

The South-West was a part of the country that I wasn't all that familiar with at the time, but once we'd gone to visit a few times, we found it to be the ideal place to raise our children

After making a few leisurely visits, the need to find appropriate accommodation became pressing. We made multiple appointments with various estate agents and spent entire days looking at one house after the other. Just as time was starting to run out, we found the perfect place for a family of four.

Once we'd settled, it was time for my wife to start looking for work. Truth be told, I could tell she was getting a bit bored and thought that getting a job might raise her spirits, in addition to bringing in some extra money.

Eventually, she found a job as a supply teacher. It wasn't ideal, she'd much rather be working in one school permanently, but it was a start.

It took us a few months to get on a steady financial footing. By December, we were on an upwards curve, so we managed to have a good Christmas. At one time we hadn't thought this would be possible.

Roughly one year after we moved into our rented accommodation, our financial situation was such that we could start thinking about buying a house of our own in Plymouth. It wasn't easy to get a mortgage, and we spoke to a few banks before managing to secure the right terms.

Then we discovered another problem. Because we'd been living in rented accommodation for so long, we hadn't bought any furniture of our own. So we saved up some money, so that when the time came, we could furnish our house in style.

We arranged for the new furniture to be delivered on the same day that we moved into our new house. By the time the removal men had left, each room smelt of new furniture.

The Monday following our move, both my wife and I took our new, shorter routes to work. It was like that day marked the beginning of something new. This was the day when we started to rebuild our lives.

Chapter 19

Once we'd settled into our new home in Plymouth, everything went smoothly. I had a good, well-paying job, my wife was happy in her work and my daughters thrived in their new school.

Sometimes my daughters said they missed their old friends and my wife mentioned the odd thing too, but on the whole, none of us doubted that we'd made the right decision. For the first time in our married lives, we could relax, knowing there was no one looking over our shoulders, waiting for the perfect moment to accuse me of being a troublemaker

As happy as we were, I did get homesick. I didn't mention it to my wife at first, so as not to unsettle her. Instead, I just let it fester. I wanted to see my family so much, but I knew I couldn't.

I never have been able to hide anything from my wife. She noticed my subdued demeanour and demanded to know what was troubling me. I kept on denying anything was wrong, until one day, she guessed correctly. She gave me many kind words and was very sympathetic. She agreed that I had to go home and see my family, but knew, as I did, that it would be hazardous. We talked for a long time, trying to come up with possible solutions to the problem. In the end, it was her idea to visit a neighbouring country.

I gave it some thought, forming the conclusion that this was the best option open to me, but I'd need to contact my brother first, to gain some insights into the political situation. I suppose, deep down, I was hoping he'd say that things were not as bad as I'd imagined, and that it would be safe for me to travel to Iraq. I was wrong.

He gave me an overview of the situation, which I found most useful. There were sanctions on the import of foods and medicines. Everyone was much poorer than before, because there was no longer any revenue from the export of oil. For many people, the situation was dire. The elderly, babies and children were the hardest hit

This came as a great shock. I knew from the way he was talking that it wouldn't be safe for me to travel home, but I decided to ask anyway. I thought it would be good to hear someone say it or else there'd be a one per cent chance things would be OK, and it would be forever praying on my mind.

He said that I shouldn't travel back home, not under any circumstances. If I did, I'd most likely be killed. My worst fears had been confirmed. Feeling utterly deflated, I suggested to him that we meet up in a neighbouring country.

There was a moment's silence whilst, I assumed, he gave the matter some thought. It was a good idea by all accounts. He sounded enthusiastic at first, which then turned to excitement. He was obviously as elated as I was that we'd found a solution and we would shortly be able to meet.

After relaying this information back to my wife, she urged me caution. She said it sounded like a good idea and agreed that I had to take a risk, but pleaded with me to be careful. I promised her this and then started making preparations.

We decided it would be best if I travel to neighbouring Amman and Damascus. It was safe territory, even for an Iraqi national, but it didn't stop me from worrying. In this part of the world, you never knew who was watching you.

Therefore, it was a nervy flight, during which I hardly said a word to anyone. At first, my thoughts were occupied with my wife and daughters, the way they'd stood waving at me as I'd boarded the plane. I wasn't going to be away for long, but I was already missing them.

As time passed, and I became more and more uncomfortable in the cramped-up seat, I started to mull over the past. I thought about the first time I'd travelled back from the UK, after completing my studies. The way I'd been worried about breaking the news of my engagement to an English woman to my parents. This was a happy memory to begin with that made me smile, but then I thought a lot about my parents and a tear came to my eye.

Although Hussein wasn't going to be there, part of me still thought he would be. My subconscious kept telling me this was a dream and any minute I'd wake up to find him laughing and joking at my bedside.

That moved my train of thought on to the last time I'd seen him. The person in the hospital bed wasn't the Hussein I knew, or the one I chose to remember. I recalled how he'd said he wanted his children to be taken care of. Although I hadn't seen him for a while, I knew my brother would be doing a splendid job in that respect. I made it my mission to find out as much about them as I possibly could.

As the plane began its descent, I imagined a guard walking through the crowd with a gun and a pair of handcuffs. Then it occurred to me that

331

Dr Mosa Abu Rgheff

if this actually happened, I wouldn't be seeing any of my family again, not for a long time. Maybe not ever.

The glass doors parted, and I entered the terminal. Straight away, I noticed something strange in my periphery. I dismissed it to begin with, and continued walking happily on my way. Then I saw him again, at roughly 3 o'clock. I turned to seek out whoever it was that was finding me so interesting. Given everything I'd been through, it wouldn't have surprised me if I was being watched, not at all. He saw me looking and quickly turned his head. At that point, I knew something was wrong.

All the time I was in the airport, I kept on imagining someone was watching me, boring a hole in my back with his eyes.

As soon as I set eyes on my brother, the man slipped from my mind. It was some time before I thought about him again. I glanced around the terminal, trying to remain inconspicuous, but there was nothing. I decided it had all been a figment of my imagination and proceeded to leave the airport with my brother. With one foot through the glass doors, I couldn't resist looking over my shoulder one more time. And there he was, heading straight for my brother and I. As he approached, I saw he was a harmless elderly gentleman. At last, I could relax.

We all stayed at the same hotel to make it easy for us to enjoy each other's company. We spent that first night catching up and generally enjoying a few laughs. They were all interested to hear about my family, which was reciprocated enthusiastically. I thought about asking about Hussein's children there and then, but decided to leave that for the next day when I was not tired from the flight and when there was more time to absorb all their news.

Shortly after breakfast, I sat on the end of my brother's bed, listening to his news, fascinated. When the sound of passing cars and people in the corridor filled up the room, I decided it was time to talk about Hussein.

Needless to say, they were all as emotional as I was. We spoke about our childhood, his studies and the things he did to make us laugh. No one mentioned his time in detention or his death. This was a time for remembering the positive things about him, like he was there making us laugh in the room.

Waiting for a break in the conversation, I asked about Hussein's children. "What about his family, are they OK? His children doing well at school?"

"Oh, they're doing fine, thriving in fact."

"Tell me more."

My brother produced some copies of their school reports from his bag. As I hadn't explicitly requested him to do this, I marvelled at the way he, along with the rest of my family, knew what to do at precisely the right time. I was lucky to be part of a family where we all knew each other so well.

He passed them to me, and I spent a long while examining them in as much detail as I do my students' papers.

Hussein's children were doing excellently, my brother was right. They were all top of their classes. They were obviously highly intelligent, even more so than I'd given them credit for.

"This is great news," I said, passing the reports back to my brother.

My brother smiled and said he agreed. I can't overstate how much this pleased me. Hussein's life had been cut short in such terrible circumstances, but his spirit was living on. Not for the first time that day, it felt like he was there, in the room with us.

Back in the UK, I was still feeling elated from the news I'd been given. More than any other time I'd visited, it felt like my mission had been accomplished.

My wife was as delighted as I had been when I gave her the news. She said she'd like to accompany me next time, but I reminded her that, for the moment, it wasn't safe. Reluctantly, she accepted this, but I could tell from her subdued expression that she was feeling both frustrated and disappointed.

Throughout the 1990s, I met with my siblings regularly, but never in Iraq. I was glad to hear news of my nephews and nieces, but, secretly, I was always more interested in Hussein's children. It didn't surprise me at all to hear that they were destined for the top, academically.

As time passed, I began to feel more and more at home in the UK. Finally, we could live the life we'd always wanted, without having to continually look over our shoulders. Everything seemed to centre around our daughters, who were living through their teenage years. By the end of the decade, they'd completed the transformation into adulthood, making everyone very proud.

This didn't mean that I ever stopped wanting to go home, however. It's just that up until 2003 when the regime was toppled, it just wasn't safe.

On one occasion, Saddam's son in law escaped to neighbouring Jordan, where he spoke up against the regime. Saddam sent word to his son in law that he'd forgiven him. But this was a trap. Saddam sent his own son to meet his son in law at the checkpoint to issue his arrest. As soon at they arrived home, his son in law was killed.

If Saddam could do this to a member of his own family, what chance did I have? Not only had I been perceived as a troublemaker for most of my adult life, but I'd broken the terms of my visa and remained in the UK.

In 2003, everything changed, both in the UK and Iraq. Saddam was finally toppled, and the regime banished, which opened up many new opportunities. But I still didn't consider it safe for my family to travel with me. Not only that, the sanctions on food and medicines that the UN had imposed back in 1990, were still in place. I didn't want to run the risk of them falling ill and there being no medicines available. Nor did I want them to go hungry or suffer the indignity of having to queue up to beg for food. I decided to wait until the sanctions had been lifted, whenever that might be. I was delighted and relieved when the wait came to an end shortly after the regime had been toppled. I put plans in place to go home alone.

One particularly poignant visit came in 2004. I flew to Amman, where I was met by my nephew and his family, before journeying home in a taxi. I'd been following every news report for the last year or so, and now I wanted to see for myself how the people were coping, especially my family, both inner and extended.

I arrived home to find my nephews, nieces, along with everyone else, there to meet me. Catching up with people that I loved dearly, and whom I hadn't seen for almost 14 years, was enough to bring a tear to my eye. It was like a part of my tortured soul had finally been relieved of its burden.

I spent the next few days, mainly in the company of my siblings and their families. We spoke a lot about the old days. Although I enjoyed English cuisine and my wife was a great cook, it was good to eat some traditional dishes again. I just hoped it wouldn't leave me pining for something unobtainable when I got back to England.

Once I'd met everyone at least twice, I started to think about my parents and what they'd say if they could see us now. I felt the urge to go and visit them in Najaf, which is just south of Baghdad, where they, along with Hussein, had been interred.

I placed a bouquet of flowers on each of their graves and sat down to think. It was good to have the opportunity to talk to them after all those years. I had so much to say that it was hard to know where to begin.

As I sat there, tears stinging my eyes in the bright sun, I had a series of flashbacks. First, I saw a vision of my father. He was taking me to my place of birth to get the documents that were necessary for my university application. It was so vivid that I wanted to reach out and touch him, to tell him how much I miss him and that he was the best father anyone could hope to have. I wanted to say to him that the documents were also necessary for my overseas travel, which I don't think he knew. As the image faded, a tear came to my eye. My thoughts then turned to my mother, who also appeared in a vision.

From what I could make out, it was the night before my flight to Heathrow, in September

1962. Yes, that's when it was. She was saying how proud she felt, but appeared to be a bit confused as to where I was actually going. This made me laugh, as it had at the time.

Then it was the turn of my elder brother. He was running towards me at the airport. It was on my return from the UK. He was running so fast that he was out of breath, but that didn't stop him from telling me loud and clear that he'd heard on the radio that I'd been invited for an interview—for a scholarship to study abroad. My dad was with him too, smiling. He patted me on the back and said well done.

As that vision faded, another appeared, just as vivid as the others. It was of Hussein, in his hospital bed. But he wasn't oblivious to what was going on around him as he had been in reality. He was sat up, smiling, laughing, and joking with his family, who were all gathered around his bed. I could clearly hear what each of them was saying, down to the tiniest detail. This affected me more than the other visions. I wished it could have happened this way.

I stood up and took a step closer, until the tips of my toes almost touched the flowers I'd laid. I wanted to get something off my chest, something I'd been wanting to say for years, going back to when they were alive. I loved them so much, and I had to let them know.

I had never really forgiven myself for causing them so much pain and anguish when I was younger. I asked them to forgive me for this.

I told them that they were grandparents to four lovely children, who had lit up the lives of everyone that knew them.

Then I moved to Hussein's stone and lowered my head, just as I had for my parents'. He had to know how well his children had done in life. I knew from the type of character he was and from the way his children had turned out, that they would have been his world. He'd have loved them more than anything.

But this wasn't enough. If he was there with me, he'd have asked for every minute detail of their lives to date, so I told him. I said, "The little boy that was with you when you fell at the front door, graduated with a degree in production engineering. Your other son graduated with a degree in computer engineering, and the son you never had chance to see graduated with a degree in medicine.

"Your daughters have done just as well, my dear brother. One has graduated with a degree in science, the other with a degree in electrical engineering. And your daughter with one or two health issues—she hasn't let her disadvantages hold her back. She had to be educated at home though, but only because there were no special needs schools in town."

"My brother, all your family have done so well in your absence. They couldn't have turned out any better. They are perfect, both as children and as people. Just like you.

I wiped my eyes and made the slow walk back to my car. I felt determined to go home again, at the next available opportunity. It was a sombre flight back to the UK, but when my wife saw me, she knew straight away that now I'd said everything I'd been meaning to, I felt lighter and happier than I had for years.

Epiloge

The number of people around the world being abused, tortured and brutally killed without a fair trial, continues to rise year on year. These crimes are overseen by totalitarian rulers, who are more abundant than you might think.

Before I put pen to paper, I paused to consider what differentiates my life from the many others suffering behind closed doors, and what could the reader take away from my story?

In an attempt to answer this question, I have detailed my achievements, endeavours, and experiences between the painful past and future juncture. Despite my brush with death, I never lost sight of my ambitions, and I remained as determined as ever to see them realised.

I, like many other Iraqi scholars at UK universities, was ambitious to build the Iraqi dream; freedom, respect for human rights, and better living standards for all. However, the regime tried to quash our aspirations and determination to succeed using methods that can only be described as barbaric. Most highly-skilled engineers and scientists had to leave their country. Some lost their lives at the hands of a ruler with no morals.

Saddam used fear rather than logic as a means to gain power. He was the first ruler in recent history to order targeted killing of citizens who questioned his legitimacy or policies. Yet in the 2003 invasion, few fought to keep him in power. His removal was welcomed by almost everyone. It opened avenues for scientists, engineers and other highly skilled people to rebuild a country that had been destroyed by his wars and the invasion. But since 2003, the country has been plagued by civil war.

Dictators control the citizens, and rule by force. But citizens can survive, providing they heed to the lesson that perseverance and self-sacrifices are more important than the rule of fear. Saddam didn't listen to reason or peaceful debate. He ruled the country for three decades, and by the time he was executed, he was in his 70s. His rule collapsed miserably. He'd caused much pain to his family and destroyed the country of his own birth.

So, referring back to the question of what you, the reader, can take away from my story, I refer to the Latin phrase 'nil carborundum illegitimi', which, translated into contemporary language, means 'don't let the bastards grind you down'.

Our children have now completed their education. Our eldest attained a PhD from a university in London and our younger a degree in art. Both are married, with two children each. My wife and I have four grandchildren; 4 beautiful girls and 1 grandson. Like their parents, they have joined the teaching profession.

Since we moved to the UK, I, personally, have lived without fear. Furthermore, there have been vital opportunities to network with like-minded international academics and researchers. This has empowered me to proliferate an outstanding academic record in wireless communications, including a wealth of research applications, which have been published in renowned journals. In addition, my research has been presented in distinguished international conferences. Further, I have written 2 engineering books. The first of these, about 3G technology, was published in 2007 by Academic press. The second, released in late 2019 by Wiley and IEEE Press, detailed my research into 5G technologies. I have also had a patent on wireless technology. More recently, I have written several technical articles on the applications of 5G networks.

I have visited my family several times over the years, but always without my wife and family. The country is still considered a high risk to visit. I have to keep on disappointing my grandchildren when they ask to go and see the historical places I describe to them. I hope that some day we'll be able to make the trip together.

Printed in Great Britain
by Amazon